RELIGION WITHOUT GOD

RELIGION

WITHOUT

GOD

Ronald Dworkin

WITHDRAWN

HARVARD UNIVERSITY PRESS

Cambridge, Massachusetts, and London, England

2013

Library of Congress Cataloging-in-Publication Data

Dworkin, Ronald.
Religion without god / Ronald Dworkin.
pages   cm
"Based on the Einstein Lectures that Ronald Dworkin
delivered at the University of Bern in December 2011."
Includes bibliographical references and index.
ISBN 978-0-674-72682-6 (alk. paper)
1. Religion—Philosophy.   2. Atheism.   3. Freedom
of religion.   I. Title.
BL51.D96   2013
200—dc23   2013020724

To Tom—who led me into the mysteries
of the secular temperament

———————

And to Reni—forever

CONTENTS

PUBLISHER'S NOTE

THIS BOOK IS BASED on the Einstein Lectures that Ronald Dworkin delivered at the University of Bern in December 2011. He planned to greatly extend his treatment of the subject over the next few years, but he became ill in the summer of 2012 and had time only to complete some revisions of the original text before his death in February 2013. The publisher would like to thank Hillary Nye, a doctoral student at the NYU School of Law, for valuable research assistance in preparing the book for publication. Professor Dworkin's research was supported by the NYU School of Law's Filomen D'Agostino and Max E. Greenberg Foundation.

RELIGION WITHOUT GOD

underwrites value, however, as I will argue, presupposes a prior commitment to the independent reality of that value. That commitment is available to nonbelievers as well. So theists share a commitment with some atheists that is more fundamental than what divides them, and that shared faith might therefore furnish a basis for improved communication between them.

The familiar stark divide between people of religion and without religion is too crude. Many millions of people who count themselves as atheists have convictions and experiences similar to and just as profound as those that believers count as religious. They say that though they do not believe in a "personal" god, they nevertheless believe in a "force" in the universe "greater than we are." They feel an inescapable responsibility to live their lives well, with due respect for the lives of others; they take pride in a life they think well lived and suffer sometimes inconsolable regret at a life they think, in retrospect, wasted. They find the Grand Canyon not just arresting but breathtakingly and eerily wonderful. They are not simply interested in the latest discoveries about vast space but enthralled by them. These are not, for them, just a matter of immediate sensuous and otherwise inexplicable response. They express a conviction that the force and wonder they sense are real, just as real as planets or pain, that moral truth and natural wonder do not simply evoke awe but call for it.

There are famous and poetic expressions of the same set of attitudes. Albert Einstein said that though an atheist he was a deeply religious man.

> To know that what is impenetrable to us really exists, manifesting itself as the highest wisdom and the most radiant beauty which our dull faculties can comprehend only in their most primitive forms—this knowledge, this feeling, is at the center of true religiousness. In this sense, and in this sense only, I belong in the ranks of devoutly religious men.[1]

Percy Bysshe Shelley declared himself an atheist who nevertheless felt "The awful shadow of some unseen Power / Floats though unseen among us."[2] Philosophers, historians, and sociologists of religion have insisted on an account of religious experience that finds a place for religious atheism. William James said that one of the two essentials of religion is a sense of fundamentality: that there are "things in the universe," as he put it, "that throw the last stone."[3] Theists have a god for that role, but an atheist can think that the importance of living well throws the last stone, that there is nothing more basic on which that responsibility rests or needs to rest.

Judges often have to decide what "religion" means for legal purposes. For example, the US Supreme Court had to decide whether, when Congress provided a "conscientious objection" exemption from military service for men whose religion would not allow them to serve, an atheist whose moral convictions also prohibited service qualified for the objection. It decided that he did qualify.[4] The Court, called upon to interpret the Constitution's guarantee of "free exercise of religion" in another case, declared that many religions flourish in the United States that do not recognize a god, including something the Court called

"secular humanism."[5] Ordinary people, moreover, have come to use "religion" in contexts having nothing to do with either gods or ineffable
forces. They say that Americans make a religion of
their Constitution, and that for some people base-
ball is a religion. These latter uses of the term "religion" are only metaphorical, to be sure, but they
seem parasitic not on beliefs about God but rather
on deep commitments more generally.

So the phrase "religious atheism," however surprising, is not an oxymoron; religion is not restricted
to theism just as a matter of what words mean. But
the phrase might still be thought confusing. Would
it not be better, for the sake of clarity, to reserve
"religion" for theism and then to say that Einstein,
Shelley, and the others are "sensitive" or "spiritual"
atheists? But on a second look, expanding the terri-
tory of religion improves clarity by making plain
the importance of what is shared across that terri-
tory. Richard Dawkins says that Einstein's language
is "destructively misleading"[6] because clarity demands a sharp distinction between a belief that the
universe is governed by fundamental physical laws,

level from national elections to local school board meetings. The fiercest battles are then not between different sects of godly religion but between zealous believers and those atheists they regard as immoral heathens who cannot be trusted and whose growing numbers threaten the moral health and integrity of the political community.

The zealots have great political power in America now, at least for the present. The so-called religious right is a voting bloc still eagerly courted. The political power of religion has provoked, predictably, an opposite—though hardly equal—reaction. Militant atheism, though politically inert, is now a great commercial success. No one who called himself an atheist could be elected to any important office in America, but Richard Dawkins's book *The God Delusion* (2006) has sold millions of copies, and dozens of other books that condemn religion as superstition crowd American bookstores. Books ridiculing God were once, decades ago, rare. Religion meant a Bible, and no one thought it worth the trouble to point out the endless errors of the biblical account of creation. No more. Scholars devote careers to refuting what once seemed, among those who enthusiastically buy their books, too silly to refute.

If we can separate God from religion—if we can come to understand what the religious point of view really is and why it does not require or assume a supernatural person—then we may be able to lower, at least, the temperature of these battles by separating questions of science from questions of value. The new religious wars are now really culture wars. They are not just about scientific history—about what best accounts for the development of the human species, for instance—but more fundamentally about the meaning of human life and what living well means. As we shall see, logic requires a separation between the scientific and value parts of orthodox godly religion. When we separate these properly, we discover that they are fully independent: the value part does not depend—cannot depend—on any god's existence or history. If we accept this, then we formidably shrink both the size and the importance of the wars. They would no longer be culture wars. This ambition is utopian: violent and nonviolent religious wars re-flect hatreds deeper than philosophy can address. But a little philosophy might help.

What Is Religion? The Metaphysical Core

What, then, should we count as a religious atti-tude? I will try to provide a reasonably abstract and hence ecumenical account. The religious attitude accepts the full, independent reality of value. It accepts the objective truth of two central judg-ments about value. The first holds that human life has objective meaning or importance. Each per-son has an innate and inescapable responsibility to try to make his life a successful one: that means living well, accepting ethical responsibilities to oneself as well as moral responsibilities to others, not just if we happen to think this important but because it is in itself important whether we think so or not. The second holds that what we call "nature"—the universe as a whole and in all its parts—is not just a matter of fact but is itself sub-lime: something of intrinsic value and wonder.

Together these two comprehensive value judgments declare inherent value in both dimensions of human life: biological and biographical. We are part of nature because we have a physical being and duration: nature is the locus and nutrient of our physical lives. We are apart from nature because we are conscious of ourselves as making a life and must make decisions that, taken together, determine what life we have made.

For many people religion includes much more than those two values: for many theists it also includes obligations of worship, for instance. But I shall take these two—life's intrinsic meaning and nature's intrinsic beauty—as paradigms of a fully religious attitude to life. These are not convictions that one can isolate from the rest of one's life. They engage a whole personality. They permeate experience: they generate pride, remorse, and thrill. Mystery is an important part of that thrill. William James said, "Like love, like wrath, like hope, ambition, jealousy, like every other instinctive eagerness and impulse, [religion] adds to life an enchantment which is not rationally or logically deducible from anything else."[8] The enchantment is the discovery of transcendental value in what seems otherwise transient and dead.

But how can religious atheists know what they claim about the various values they embrace? How can they be in touch with the world of value to check the perhaps fanciful claim in which they invest so much emotion? Believers have the authority of a god for their convictions; atheists seem to pluck theirs out of the air. We need to explore a bit the metaphysics of value.[9]

The religious attitude rejects naturalism, which is one name for the very popular metaphysical theory that nothing is real except what can be studied by the natural sciences, including psychology. That is, nothing exists that is neither matter nor mind; there is really, fundamentally, no such thing as a good life or justice or cruelty or beauty. Richard Dawkins spoke for naturalists when he suggested the scientists' proper reply to people who, criticizing naturalism, endlessly quote Hamlet: "There are more things in heaven and earth, Horatio, than are dreamt of in your philosophy." "Yes," Dawkins replied, "but we're working on it."[10]

Some naturalists are nihilists: they say that values are only illusions. Other naturalists accept that in some sense values exist, but they define them so as to deny them any independent existence: they make them depend entirely on people's thoughts or reactions. They say, for instance, that describing someone's behavior as good or right only means that, as a matter of fact, the lives of more people will be pleasant if everyone behaves in that way. Or that saying a painting is beautiful only means that in general people take pleasure in looking at it.

The religious attitude rejects all forms of naturalism. It insists that values are real and fundamental, not just manifestations of something else; they are as real as trees or pain. It also rejects a very different theory we might call grounded realism. This position, also popular among philosophers, holds that values are real and that our value judgments can be objectively true—but only on the assumption, which might be wrong, that we have good reason, apart from our own confidence in our value judgments, to think that we have the capacity to discover truths about value.

There are many forms of grounded realism: one is a form of theism that traces our capacity for value judgment to a god. (I shall shortly argue that this supposed grounding goes in the wrong direction.) They all agree that, if value judgment can ever be sound, there must be some independent reason to think that people have a capacity for sound moral judgment—independent because it does not itself rely on that capacity. That makes the status of value hostage to biology or metaphysics. Suppose we find undeniable evidence that we hold the moral convictions we do only because they were evolutionarily adaptive, which certainly did not require them to be true. Then, on this view, we would have no reason to think that cruelty is really wrong. If we think it is, then we must think we have some other way of being "in touch with" moral truth.

The religious attitude insists on a much more fundamental divorce between the world of value and facts about our natural history or our psychological susceptibilities. Nothing could impeach our judgment that cruelty is wrong except a good moral argument that cruelty is not after all wrong. We ask: What reason do we have for supposing that we have the capacity for sound value judgment? Ungrounded realism answers: The only possible reason we could have—we reflect responsibly on our moral convictions and find them persuasive. We think them true, and we therefore think we have the capacity to find the truth. How can we reject the hypothesis that all our convictions about value are only mutually supporting illusions? Ungrounded realism answers: We understand that hypothesis in the only way that makes it intelligible. It suggests that we do not have an adequate moral case for any of our moral judgments. We refute that suggestion by making moral arguments for some of our moral judgments.

The religious attitude, to repeat, insists on the full independence of value: the world of value is self-contained and self-certifying. Does that disqualify the religious attitude on grounds of circularity? Notice that there is no finally noncircular way to certify our capacity to find truth of any kind in any intellectual domain. We rely on experiment and observation to certify our judgments in science. But experiment and observation are reliable only in virtue of the truth of basic assumptions about causation and optics that we rely on science itself, and nothing more basic, to certify. And of course our judgments about the nature of the external world all depend, even more fundamentally, on a universally shared assumption that there is an external world, an assumption that science cannot itself certify.

We find it impossible not to believe the elementary truths of mathematics and, when we understand them, the astonishingly complex truths that mathematicians have proved. But we cannot demonstrate either the elementary truths or the methods of mathematical demonstration from outside mathematics. We feel that we do not need any independent certification: we know we have an innate capacity for logic and mathematical truth. But how do we know we have that capacity? Only because we form beliefs in these domains that we simply cannot, however we try, disown. So we must have such a capacity.

We might say: We accept our most basic scientific and mathematical capacities finally as a matter of faith. The religious attitude insists that we embrace our values in the same way: finally as a matter of faith as well. There is a striking difference. We have generally agreed standards of good scientific argument and valid mathematical demonstration, but no agreed standards for moral or other forms of reasoning about value. On the contrary, we disagree markedly about goodness, right, beauty, and justice. Does that mean that we have an external certification of our capacities for science and mathematics that we lack in the domain of value?

No, because interpersonal agreement is not an external certification in any domain. The

principles of scientific method, including the need
for interpersonal confirmation of observation, are
justified only by the science these methods have
produced. As I said, everything in science, including the importance of shared observation,
hangs together: it rests on nothing outside science itself. Logic and mathematics are different
still. Consensus about the validity of a complex
mathematical argument is in no way *evidence* of
that validity. What if—unimaginable horror—the
human race ceased to agree about valid mathematical or logical arguments? It would fall into
terminal decline, but no one would have any good
reason, along the way, to doubt that five and seven
make twelve. Value is different still. If value is
objective, then consensus about a particular value
judgment is irrelevant to its truth or anyone's responsibility in thinking it true, and experience
shows, for better or worse, that the human community can survive great discord about moral or
ethical or aesthetic truth. For the religious attitude, disagreement is a red herring.

I said, just now, that the religious attitude rests
finally on faith. I said that mainly to point out

that science and mathematics are, in the same way, matters of faith as well. In each domain we accept felt, inescapable conviction rather than the benediction of some independent means of verification as the final arbiter of what we are entitled responsibly to believe. This kind of faith is not just passive acceptance of the conceptual truth that we cannot justify our science or our logic or our values without appealing to science or logic or value. It is a positive affirmation of the reality of these worlds and of our confidence that though each of our judgments may be wrong, we are entitled to think them right if we have reflected on them responsibly enough.

In the special case of value, however, faith means something more, because our convictions about value are emotional commitments as well and, whatever tests of coherence and internal support they survive, they must also feel right in an emotional way. They must have a grip on one's whole personality. Theologians often say that religious faith is a sui generis experience of conviction. Rudolf Otto, in a markedly influential book, called the experience "numinous"[11] and said it was a kind of "faith-knowledge." I mean to suggest that convictions of value are also complex, sui generis, emotional experiences. We will see in Chapter 2 that when scientists confront the unimaginable vastness of space and the astounding complexity of atomic particles, they have an emotional reaction that matches Otto's description surprisingly well. Indeed, many of them use the very term "numinous" to describe what they feel. They find the universe awe-inspiring and deserving of a kind of emotional response that at least borders on trembling.

But of course I do not mean, in speaking of faith, that the fact that a moral conviction survives reflection is itself an argument for that conviction. A conviction of truth is a psychological fact, and only a value judgment can argue for the conviction's truth. And of course I do not mean that value judgments are in the end only subjective. Our felt conviction that cruelty is wrong is a conviction that cruelty is really wrong; we cannot have that conviction without thinking that it is objectively true. Acknowledging the role of atheism. We hope better to understand why so many people declare that they have a sense of value, mystery, and purpose in life in spite of their atheism rather than in addition to their atheism: why they associate their values with those of conventional religion in that way. We also hope to produce an account of religion that we can use to interpret the widespread conviction that people have special rights to religious freedom: that is the project of Chapter 3. I want now to explore another, more complex, reason for treating the attitude I describe as religious. Theists assume that their value realism is grounded realism. God, they think, has provided and certifies their perception of value: of the responsibilities of life and the wonders of the universe. In fact, however, their realism must finally be ungrounded. It is the radical independence of value from history, including divine history, that makes their faith defensible.

The heart of my argument is the following assumption. The conventional, theistic religions with which most of us are most familiar—Judaism,

Some of these are godly commitments—that is, commitments that are parasitic on and make no sense without the assumption of a god. Godly convictions declare duties of worship, prayer, and obedience to the god the religion endorses. But other religious values are not, in that way, godly: they are at least formally independent of any god. The two paradigm religious values I identified are in that way independent. Religious atheists do not believe in a god and so reject the science of conventional religions and the godly commitments, like a duty of ritual worship, that are dependent on that part. But they accept that it matters objectively how a human life goes and that everyone has an innate, inalienable ethical responsibility to try to live as well as possible in his circumstances. They accept that nature is not just a matter of particles thrown together in a very long history but something of intrinsic wonder and beauty.

The science part of conventional religion cannot ground the value part because—to put it briefly at first—these are conceptually independent. Human life cannot have any kind of meaning or value just because a loving god exists. The universe cannot be intrinsically beautiful just because it was created to be beautiful. Any judgment about meaning in human life or wonder in nature relies ultimately not only on descriptive truth, no matter how exalted or mysterious, but finally on more fundamental value judgments. There is no direct bridge from any story about the creation of the firmament, or the heavens and earth, or the animals of the sea and the land, or the delights of heaven, or the fires of hell, or the parting of any sea or the raising of any dead, to the enduring value of friendship and family or the importance of charity or the sublimity of a sunset or the appropriateness of awe in the face of the universe or even a duty of reverence for a creator god.

I do not argue in this book against the science of the traditional Abrahamic religions. I do not argue that there is no personal god who made the heavens and loves its creatures. I claim only that such a god's existence cannot in itself make a difference to the truth of any religious values. If a god exists, perhaps he can send people to heaven or hell. But he cannot of his own will create right answers to moral questions or instill the universe with a glory it would not otherwise have. A god's existence or character can figure in the defense of such values only as a fact that makes some different, independent background value judgment pertinent; it can figure only, that is, as a minor premise. Of course, a belief in a god can shape a person's life dramatically. Whether and how it does this depends on the character of the supposed god and the depth of commitment to that god. An obvious and crude case: someone who believes he will go to hell if he displeases a god will very likely lead a different life from someone who does not have any such belief. But whether what displeases a god is morally wrong is not up to that god.

I am now relying on an important conceptual principle that we might call "Hume's principle" because it was defended by that eighteenth-century Scottish philosopher.[12] This principle insists that one cannot support a value judgment—an ethical or moral or aesthetic claim—just by a pertinent background moral principle to have any impact on value judgments. That is important because those background value judgments can themselves be defended—to the extent they can be defended at all—only by locating them in a larger network of values each of which draws on and justifies the others. They can be defended, as my account of the religious attitude insists, only within the overall scheme of value.

So a god's existence can be shown to be either necessary or sufficient to justify a particular conviction of value only if some independent background principle explains why. We might well be convinced of some such principle. We might think, for instance, that the sacrifice of God's son on the cross gives us a responsibility of gratitude to honor the principles for which he died. Or that we owe the deference to the god who created us that we owe a parent, except that our deference to that god must be unlimited and unstinting. Believers will have no trouble constructing other such principles. But the principles they cite, whatever they are, must have independent force seen only as claims of morality or some other department of value. Theists must have an independent faith in some such principle; it is that principle, rather than just the divine events or other facts they claim pertinent, that they must find they cannot but believe. What divides godly and godless religion—the science of godly religion—is not as important as the faith in value that unites them.

Mystery and Intelligibility

Sophisticated theologians will no doubt regard my argument as ignorant and puerile. In their view I have taken a familiar set of assumptions about the relationship between fact and value that make sense in our ordinary terrestrial lives and tried to apply those assumptions to a celestial realm in which they do not make sense. I must therefore emphasize the narrowness of my assumptions. I am not assuming that all believers accept the biblical account of creation as literally true. I accept that some theologians' conceptions of divine creation, if we can make sense of this at all, would be radically unlike any form of creation with which we are familiar. I know that many theologians believe that the character of such creation is mysterious and may be beyond any human power to explain.

But it seems a minimal requirement of any theistic conception that divine creation, whatever else it is, be an act of intelligent agency. It is hard to see what would be left of theism if some form of creative agency did not form part of its science. So the challenge to those who find my argument ignorant, I believe, is this: Is there an intelligible, even if unfamiliar, conception of agency from which it follows that its exercise can in and by itself create value? The religious attitude as I described it holds that events cannot in themselves automatically make judgments of value true: some background assumption of value is needed that makes the event an argument for the truth of that judgment. That conceptual principle cannot be overcome by stipulating that divine represented by the Greek gods of Olympus. They were immortal human beings with superhuman powers and superhuman vices: they were vain, jealous, vengeful, and otherwise terrible. The pagan gods were replaced, in the burgeoning Abrahamic religions, by one god, the Sistine God, the bearded figure creating life on the ceiling and, in the person of his son, sending people to heaven and hell on the back wall. It is the Sistine God who dominates practicing theism today: he is omniscient and all-powerful and takes enormous interest in the lives of those he has created. In the seventeenth century a different kind of god emerged, though never with a very large constituency. The bookmark God explains what science cannot: he does not intervene in human affairs, as the Sistine God does, but he is available to explain the existence and character of the universe so far as science has not yet explained it. He does not challenge the now-reigning story of evolution, for example; on the contrary, he set evolution up so that over eons it would do what it has. He moves back in the book of knowledge as science writes more pages.

All these gods, even the bookmark God, are personal gods. But some people say that they believe in an impersonal god. They don't mean that their god is impersonal in the way that people can be impersonal: aloof in their manner, for instance. They mean that their god is not a person at all. We might well ask: What would a godly nonperson be like? What is the difference between a god that is not a person and no god at all? We assume that a personal god has all the capacities of a recognizable person—in particular that he has a mind, a will, and a set of purposes that he exercises his will to carry out. He has these capacities to an unimaginably powerful degree; those who believe in a personal god cannot imagine an even greater intelligence or an even more efficacious will. But intellect, purpose, and will are attributes of a person—there can be no purpose without a person whose purpose it is—and perfection of intellect, will, and purpose require not a nonperson but a perfect person.

So what would an impersonal god be like? We must set aside, of course, metaphorical invocations of a god. People say "God knows" in answer to a question when they mean that no one knows. Einstein often spoke of a god in that way: it was for him a kind of joke. He said that he was trying to see into the mind of God, and he asked whether God had any choice in creating the universe. The metaphors are based on a hypothetical—and for many people who speak this way, counterfactual—assumption. If a god existed, he would know, but no one else does. If a god had created the universe, would he have had any choice about which physical laws he would instill, or would he be entirely constrained by mathematical truth? These are not appeals to a nonpersonal god. On the contrary, whatever genuine metaphorical force is actually left in such expressions is plainly based on an imagined personal god.

We must turn to philosophy to find more interesting candidates for a nonpersonal god. Paul Tillich, the very influential German theologian, said that the idea of a personal god can only be understood as a symbol for something else and perhaps we should count that something else as a nonpersonal god. Here is Tillich:

> The manifestation of this ground and abyss of being and meaning creates what modern theology calls "the experience of the numinous." . . . [This] experience can occur, and occurs for the large majority of men, in connection with the impression some persons, historical or natural events, objects, words, pictures, tunes, dreams, etc. make on the human soul, creating the feeling of the holy, that is, of the presence of the "numinous." In such experiences religion lives and tries to maintain the presence of, and community with, this divine depth of our existence. But since it is "inaccessible" to any objectifying concept it must be expressed in symbols. One of these symbols is Personal God. It is the common opinion of classical theology, practically in all periods of Church history, that the predicate "personal" can be

said of the Divine only symbolically or by
analogy or if affirmed and negated at the
same time.... Without an element of "atheism" no "theism" can be maintained.[13]

Tillich's theology is very complex and it may be
unwise to focus on this single paragraph. But the
paragraph is fascinating. Religion, he says, must
proclaim the existence of a personal god, but that
proclamation must not be taken at face value. It
offers the idea of a personal god only as a gesture
toward what cannot be described, a gesture that
is appropriate only if the god it proclaims is at the
same moment denied. He did not mean that a
personal god is a symbol for something that
might more accurately be called a nonpersonal
god. He meant that the nerve of a religious experience can be expressed only by affirming and
denying a personal god simultaneously. He described the "numinous" character of that experience in terms that belong more to the value than
the science part of conventional religion, and
that make that experience equally available to a

religious atheist. He quoted Einstein's own reference to a "humble attitude of mind towards the grandeur of reason incarnate in existence," which, Tillich said, points

> to a common ground of the whole of the physical world and of suprapersonal values; a ground which, on the one hand, is manifest in the structure of being (the physical world) and meaning (the good, true, and beautiful), and which, on the other hand, is hidden in its inexhaustible depth.[14]

The difference between Einstein and Tillich, then, seems to come to this: they shared a kind of religious view that Einstein thought best expressed by denying a personal god and Tillich thought best expressed, though more mystically, by simultaneously denying and affirming such a god. Perhaps we should say that Tillich was both a religious theist and a religious atheist who believed that the "numinous" character of religious experience erased the difference between them.

Now turn to the even more interesting case of Baruch Spinoza. He was born in Amsterdam in 1632, into that city's Portuguese Jewish community, which had been forced out of Iberia by the Spanish Inquisition. He was excommunicated by the Amsterdam rabbinate because, they said, he was an atheist. But he actually gave something he called "God" the central, dominant place in his intricate rationalist metaphysics, and the Romantics of a later century therefore called him "god-intoxicated."

It is easy to see why Spinoza's contemporaries thought him an atheist. He denied the existence of anything that anyone within the religious community would then have been tempted to call a god. Now he is mainly read as holding, not that no god exists, but that God is coextensive with Nature. God is everything, he wrote, and everything is God. Indeed, on at least one occasion he treated "God" as just another name for Nature. So Spinoza's God is not an intelligence who stands outside everything and who, through the force of his will, has created the universe and the physical laws that govern it. His God just is the complete set of physical laws considered under a different aspect. This God does not act with purposes in mind, as the God of scripture does. Nor—to answer Einstein's joking question—does Spinoza's God have any choice about what is or will be. Because God embodies the laws of nature, God cannot act contrary to those laws. God acts mechanically and deterministically. Things all are just as they have to be.[15]

Couldn't that god be eliminated as only window dressing? If Nature, in the form of deterministic physical law, is and accounts for everything, and does this without having any ambition or plan or purpose, why bring a god into the story at all? It has been suggested that Spinoza, who lived a very private life and craved no renown or even recognition, wrote in the convoluted, crabbed way he did in hopes that only a few sympathetic readers would understand his real views. Perhaps he sprinkled God over his texts like confetti as a further disguise; to further hide his stark atheism. But that seems extremely unlikely. Spinoza was labeled an atheist anyway. And his God is not sprinkled over his arguments but sits at their core. We need a better explanation of why God is there at all.

Many scholars describe Spinoza as a "pantheist," which they take to mean just that he found God in everything. Philosophers disagree about what a pantheist is. One Spinoza scholar, Stephen Nadler, rejects that name for Spinoza on the ground that, in his view, pantheists adopt an attitude of worship for nature because it embodies their god, and Spinoza denied that any such attitude is appropriate.[16] We must take some care, however, with that suggestion. Einstein often cited Spinoza as a predecessor: he said that Spinoza's god was his god as well. Einstein did not believe in a personal god, but he did "worship" nature. He regarded it with awe and thought that he and other scientists should be humble before its beauty and mystery. He showed, that is, a religious faith in nature. Spinoza did not think the universe beautiful. He roundly denied that it is either beautiful or ugly; he thought it aesthetically inert. But he did not think it ethically or morally inert. He thought that the best way for people to live is to strive to acquire knowledge of the fundamental laws of nature. He also thought that nature is the true basis of justice and of the liberal personal and political morality he endorsed. Stuart Hampshire, an eminent Spinoza authority, described his religious attitude this way:

> What makes the moral truths true, their ground, is not to be found in the authority of God the Father and God the Son as postulated in the Christian legend, but in the structure of reality and the place of human beings within it. Their ground is to be found in the permanent constitution of reality, of how parts combine to make wholes, and therefore of how individual persons can combine to make social wholes in accordance with universal conditions of cohesion and stability.[17]

Richard Dawkins said that pantheism is only "sexed-up" atheism. I see what he meant, but "sexed-up" is very much the wrong phrase, because it suggests an advertising gimmick. Dawkins also said that when pantheists speak of God, they mean nothing more than the laws of physics. There is truth in that too, provided we understand that the pantheists he has in mind are speaking only about physical reality. Both of Dawkins's comments leave out what is crucial: the religious attitude that Spinoza and most of the people who call themselves pantheists take toward the nature they say is identical to God, or in which they say a nonpersonal god resides. Some of them describe this attitude as reflecting a "numinous" experience—an experience of sensing something nonrational and emotionally deeply moving. I quoted Tillich as using that word as well. Carl Sagan, a famous astronomer who said he did not believe in a personal god, also used "numinous" in declaring his own convictions. In the words of a commentator, Sagan meant that he "revered the universe. He was utterly imbued with awe, wonder, and a marvelous sense of belonging to a planet, a galaxy, a cosmos that inspires devotion as much as it does discovery."[18]

What Dawkins misses is that for pantheists a numinous experience is an experience of something they take to be *real*. It is not just an emotional experience whose origin and content may be explained by evolutionary advantage or by some deep psychological need. Pantheists believe there is wonder or beauty or moral truth or meaning or something else of value *in* what they experience. Their reaction is produced by a conviction of value and a response to that conviction; it cannot be accurately understood without recognizing that a real value is its object. We should not say that though pantheists—I include Spinoza—do not believe in a personal god, they believe in a nonpersonal god. It would be much clearer and more accurate to call them religious atheists. We have here another example of the value of that category. We no longer need the obscure idea of a nonpersonal god.

But the beauty we find in nature is in one way special and puzzling. You are spellbound at your first sight of the Grand Canyon. You find it awe-inspiring. Then you learn that, contrary to popular opinion, the Canyon was in fact recently created by gifted architects and artists of the Disney Corporation so that it might eventually become the site of the largest theme park the world has ever known. You might admire the artists and the ambition of the project, but the special wonder would be gone. Now think of the gorgeous flower. You learn that it is a brilliant Japanese reproduction properly indistinguishable from a real flower in odor and texture as well as color and form. You admire the skill, but once again the magic has gone. The lesson seems clear. It is not just that nature contains objects that are in themselves beautiful. Their wonder depends on the fact that it *is* nature, rather than human intelligence or skill, that has produced them.

In other contexts we value a human creation but disdain an otherwise identical object created by accident. Jackson Pollock's *Blue Poles* is overall evolutionary process endows it with a special drama. This must be that that evolutionary process and the grand universe it has created is itself a source of beauty. This thought is not available to a naturalist. Only those parts of the universe that produce pleasure in our sight can be, for him, beautiful. He finds the universe as a whole an incalculably vast accident of gas and energy. Religion finds it, on the contrary, a deep complex order shining with beauty. That conviction is ancient. It has been the firm belief of philosophers, theologians, and scientists of all epochs: Plato, Augustine, Tillich, and Einstein, for instance. Theists find it obvious why the universe is sublime: it was created to be sublime. Now we ask what reason a religious atheist might have for the same conviction.

It must, for him, begin in his science. He must rely on physics and cosmology rather than theology: science must give a religious atheist at least a glimpse of a universe fit for beauty. But the conviction of beauty is not itself science: no matter what physics reveals, about dark matter and galaxies, photons and quarks, the religious question remains. In what way is the universe that is composed of those parts beautiful? The answer to that question remains, I think, obscure. The most dramatic achievements of cosmology and particle physics have not yet described a universe that matches what religious scientists claim for it; physics has yet to reveal a universe whose beauty we can actually comprehend. So the religious conviction outstrips the science that it presumes. In that way the two branches of religion—theist and atheistic—tend to converge. They both rest, though in different ways, on faith.

I have already quoted Einstein, who said that "the center of true religiousness" is an appreciation of the "radiant beauty" of the universe. He also said this: "The most beautiful thing we can experience is the mysterious. It is the source of all true art and science. He to whom this emotion is a stranger, who can no longer pause to wonder and stand rapt in awe, is as good as dead: his eyes are closed."[1] Einstein had in mind the mysteries he had spent his life trying to unravel, and these are the mysteries that will occupy us now. I expect that "beauty" will seem to you too indiscriminate and limited a word to capture the reactions Einstein described, which include emotions of wonder, rapture, and awe. These are all different ideas, but the scientists I have read use "beauty" to cover them all, and I believe that word will serve, in all its breadth and vagueness, to cover the phenomena I mean to explore.

Einstein's faith in nature's beauty is apparently shared by most—though not all—of the physicists who work at the dramatic boundaries of their subject. Here is a small sample of the titles I found in my reading: *The Elegant Universe; Fearful Symmetry: The Search for Beauty in Modern Physics;* and *Deep Down Things: The Breathtaking Beauty of Particle Physics.*[2] Here is a sample statement of what these scientists take their mission to be, represented in the ambitions of their captain: "Einstein wanted to illuminate the workings of the universe with a clarity never before achieved, allowing us all to stand in awe of its sheer beauty and elegance."[3] There is no hint in these books that the universe is beautiful just because a god be so? Whether a theory is beautiful seems a very different question from whether it is true. But what is the alternative? Shall we say that, on the contrary, the beauty of a true scientific hypothesis is only coincidence? Would it be just a fortunate serendipity if "nature's final laws" turned out to be beautiful? But, if so, how could Weinberg think it "encouraging" that the theories now in vogue seem beautiful? Can we imagine any other role, beyond these contrary alternatives of evidence and coincidence, that the idea of beauty could play?

Second, in any case, what *kind* of beauty could Weinberg and the other physicists be thinking of? What kind of beauty can they hope to find in the dance of galaxies and quarks? We are aware of many kinds or dimensions of beauty in our terrestrial experience. Beautiful people are beautiful in a different way from beautiful buildings or chess combinations. Which of the many types of beauty can we plausibly hope to find in the cosmos or in an atom? We can have no experience of the cosmos or an atom. So what kind of beauty could we suppose these to have? We must pursue these two questions together, in tandem and in stages.

How Could Beauty Guide Research?

What role, if any, can the idea of cosmic beauty play in actual science—in research into particle physics, astrophysics, and cosmology? The simplest connection we might consider, as I just suggested, is that the beauty of a theory is evidence of its truth: that a more beautiful theory is just for that reason more likely to be true. The poet John Keats said that beauty is not just evidence, but conclusive evidence. "Beauty is truth, truth beauty," he wrote, "that is all / Ye know on earth, and all ye need to know."[5] On this view, if we have different candidates for a final theory of everything but no decisive evidence for any of them in experiment or observation, then the most beautiful among them is most likely to be true.

Naturalists would of course deny this. For them beauty cannot be evidence of truth because truth is a matter of how things are and beauty a matter only of what we choose to call beautiful. We might decide that the most beautiful theory ever invented is that the earth is held up by an elephant who stands on an infinite stack of turtles, but that would be no evidence at all that the universe is turtles all the way down. Keats's dictum was once, however, accepted by scientists devoted to the Sistine God. Beauty is evidence of truth in astronomy, they agreed, because the Sistine God is an infallible judge of beauty and would have wanted his universe to be beautiful. Circles are beautiful, so the orbits of the planets around the Sun are therefore very likely to be circular. Johannes Kepler was initially convinced of circular orbits by this argument, even though his own observations seemed to contradict his conclusion. In the end, however, he bowed to observation and changed his mind. We might say that, for him, beauty was some evidence of astronomical truth, but the evidence of observation finally overrode the evidence of beauty.

But the contemporary scientists who declare the universe beautiful do not assume that it was created by a divine artist, so they cannot take beauty to be evidence of truth for that reason. What other reason might they have? Some philosophers of science have suggested a powerful conceptual link: they say that beauty is part of the *definition* of truth in science: when physicists declare a theory true, they *mean*, among other things, that the theory is beautiful. This is an even stronger reading of Keats's claim: beauty is not just evidence of a theory's truth but part of what makes the theory true.[6] But most physicists, including most of the prominent ones, are robust realists about the physical world. They believe that the universe really is a certain way, that it is their assignment to discover how it really is, and that whether a theory is true is an entirely different question from whether it is beautiful. They do indeed prefer simple theories to complex ones and elegant theories to ungainly ones. But they think they are making a dramatic claim about reality when they say that the cosmos is beautiful. They do not think they are making only a semantic point about the definition of truth in science.

However, some great scientists are not what we might call working realists. They think it misconceives physics to suppose that physicists aim to uncover a fully mind-independent theory that exposes the universe as it really is. Stephen Hawking recently described his "model-dependent" scientific epistemology. A variety of different models might fit the observational data available at any particular moment in the development of cosmology.

> When such a model is successful at explaining events, we tend to attribute to it, and to the elements and concepts that constitute it, the quality of reality or absolute truth. But there may be different ways in which one could model the same physical situation, with each employing different fundamental elements and concepts. If two such physical theories or models accurately predict the same events, one cannot be said to be more real than the other.[7]

We adopt one model or the other, though always tentatively pending new observational evidence, on grounds that include simplicity and elegance. This "model-relative" theory of cosmic reality does indeed make beauty part of the meaning of truth in a special way: from time to time, beauty, or elegance, directs our choice about what to treat as true.

But, as I said, most physicists are working realists. They assume there is a mind-independent universe and that they must struggle to discover, so far as they can, the real truth about that universe. They cannot think either that beauty is evidence of truth or that it is part of what makes a theory true. Should we rather interpret them very differently: as meaning only that they are growing increasingly confident that the universe will turn out to be beautiful? On that view, physicists pursue their grand unifying theories according to the best scientific methods, choosing among candidate theories by asking which best survive experimental testing, and then, separately, on independent aesthetic grounds, judge the beauty of what they have discovered. It would be, on this view, a bonus if the best, last theory also, according to some such independent standard, revealed cosmic beauty. But this is just the "coincidence" it is also nearly impossible to believe it fundamentally wrong. It predicted, for instance, the discovery of a previously unknown particle, the Higgs boson, which physicists now tremulously believe, as I write, has indeed been discovered in the mammoth CERN accelerator near Geneva.

But there are problems. Perhaps the most dramatic is that the two spectacularly confirmed theories are incompatible: Einstein's theory of gravity and the standard model of the other three forces cannot both be true as absolutely general theories. Physicists dream of a "final" theory that will reconcile the two theories by finding symmetries that explain how gravity and the other forces are most fundamentally the same thing. For decades they have searched for this "quantum theory of gravity," but so far without success. Many of them speculate that the reconciliation will be found in string theory, which supposes that the universe is constructed most fundamentally of infinitesimal one-dimensional strings that vibrate in ten dimensions. But others reject that hypothesis, and none of its supporters has yet constructed a fully consistent set of equations that describe the vibrations of these strings.

The standard model offers no theoretical basis, moreover, for the properties of the particles it identifies, like their relative mass, which must be ascertained by observation and seem arbitrary. In any case, physicists now believe that 96 percent of what exists is "dark" matter and energy, which neither of the two dominant but incompatible theories offer to explain. Some of them think our universe is unique; others that it is only one of a preposterously great number of universes spread out across dimensions we cannot begin to fathom. Physicists sense and claim beauty, that is, in a totality of existence of which they are mainly ignorant. So, responsible physicists cannot suppose that they have discovered enough about the universe to feel any confidence that it is, just as a matter of coincidence, beautiful.

There is, however, a third, much more persuasive, possibility. Cosmic beauty is something different from either evidence or coincidence: it is a presumption—or rather an aspect of a presumption. The physicists who believe that the universe has great beauty also believe that it has some fundamental unity: they presume that there is, waiting to be discovered, a comprehensive, simple, and unified explanation of how the universe was born and how it works, from the largest galaxy to the tiniest particle. Weinberg describes the search for such a fundamental explanation as the "dream of a final theory." It may seem surprising, given the vast unsolved mysteries and giant uncertainties of contemporary physics, how widely that dream is shared among physicists. It is not universal among them, however. Marcelo Gleiser, for example, sets out reservations in his book *A Tear at the Edge of Creation.*[8] He suspects that the universe is finally not unified but untidy. And so he does not share the view that the universe is beautiful: he holds that only human life, not the inanimate universe, can have intrinsic value. He thinks that there is beauty in our lives and what we ourselves make, but not in the unconscious galaxies and atoms. We are wonderful, he declares, but if there is no unifying theory, there is no wonder in space itself.

This apparently strong connection between the twin presumptions—that the universe is comprehensible through a unified theory and that it is transcendently beautiful—suggests that the latter presumption is part of the former. It is *part* of the dream that the final theory will radiate that transcendent beauty. That is not itself a scientific hypothesis on a narrow empiricist conception of science. Purely scientific goals on that conception are limited to the successful explanation and prediction of everything that can be observed. In the 1960s, with the development of accelerator technology for detecting subatomic particles, a great many new, different, and apparently independent particles—leptons and gluons of different kinds—were duly discovered. Physicists complained that they had only discovered a zoo: they said that the next one of them who discovered a new particle should be fined. However, nothing in the purely scientific ambition to find a comprehensive and logically consistent explanation of everything observable rules out such a zoo. Imagine that scientists were able to compose a very long and exhaustive list of the subatomic particles they had discovered using available technology, together with a complete description of how each particle behaves in all physical contexts vis-à-vis all other particles in the list in all physical contexts. Suppose that list allowed precise prediction of observations that were repeatedly confirmed. A scientific theory must stop somewhere. Would it stain the comprehensiveness or predictive value of a perfectly consistent theory of everything to stop just at the point where every observation and prediction confirmed that theory?

We know, however, that good scientists are not content with spelling-list theories of that kind. They were dissatisfied with the zoo of particles, and their dissatisfaction generated a search for fewer, more basic particles whose properties would explain the character and behavior of the larger particles they compose. Murray Gell-Mann, whose work was groundbreaking in their discovery, called these "quarks," a name he took from

James Joyce's *Finnegans Wake*. In fact, it was necessary to recognize a substantial number of different kinds of quarks, but only a relatively few different types, so that the zoo is now much smaller. The smaller zoo is regarded as an important advance. But if quark studies do not enable more secure predictions of natural phenomena than the ugly list would, we cannot say that the explanation they provide is more comprehensive than the list would have secured. The relentless scientific search for simpler, increasingly comprehensive theories cannot be explained simply as a search for more reliable hypotheses that come closer to the truth. It must be explained as a search for beauty as well.

The explanations we rejected—that beauty is evidence of truth or part of what truth means, or that physics has already discovered enough to declare beauty by coincidence—explain in the wrong direction. Physicists find beauty in what they have so far discovered because they imagine a final, all-embracing beauty and then radiate its brilliance backward into each step toward its revelation. They call their discoveries beautiful by proxy: beautiful because they seem to hint at a yet unknown, a still mysterious, final beauty. We will next consider what kind of beauty this final beauty might be. But we should first notice that the physicists' faith, at least for a great many of them, falls naturally into a category we have constructed. It is a felt conviction that the universe really does embody a sublime beauty that does not suppose any god as a ground for that beauty. Though no doubt many physicists would reject the description, it is an example of religious atheism.

But What Kind of Beauty Could This Be?

We must try to find some match between what I called terrestrial beauty—the forms and dimensions of beauty that we encounter in our ordinary lives—and the kind of beauty we might imagine in the unseen and unseeable universe. It would plainly not do just to invent a wholly new ad hoc form of beauty: we must explain why what we hope to find is beauty as we already know it. The answer I just suggested to our first question, about the role that beauty plays in research, imposes a further condition on our search. We must find a kind or form of beauty that makes sense of the presumption of beauty I identified. It must show how it is sensible for scientists who work toward a comprehensible, fundamental, final explanation of everything to presume that that final explanation will display a magnificent beauty. Otherwise we have not really answered our first question; we have not explained the role the presumption of beauty plays in research and speculation.

We must try to satisfy these two requirements—the beauty requirement and the presumption requirement—in much the same way as we solve simultaneous mathematical equations: by finding an understanding of beauty that answers to both requirements. We might be tempted to an easy solution: that if we did find a comprehensive explanation of the whole universe, we would automatically have shown the universe to be wonderfully beautiful: it would be beautiful just because it is comprehensible. But suppose that final, comprehensive explanation was like the zoo coordinated with the dream of a final theory. We might begin by reflecting on more familiar kinds and dimensions of beauty. We can sensibly arrange these on a scale from the purely sensuous to the purely intellectual; almost everything we find beautiful has a place on that scale. No doubt there are pure cases of beautiful color sensation. But most of what we call sensuous beauty—of people, paintings, and songs—actually lies at some distance from the sensual toward the intellectual end. We perceive that beauty through a filtering lens of knowledge or supposition. That seems plainly true of architecture, poetry, and serious music: these have immediate appeal, but that appeal depends on a variety of historical and other assumptions. We find some great paintings ravishing: they command immediate sensuous response. But that response is also permeated by belief: that the painting was by Rothko, perhaps at a certain point in his career, that Rothko had certain intentions and commitments in painting as he did, and so forth. Toward the intellectual end of the scale, perception and the sensuous play less, symmetry pleasing to the eye, and that much of what we declare beautiful—the Taj Mahal and Angelina Jolie's face, for instance—exhibits a classical and attractive symmetry. We marvel at the hexagonal symmetry of a snowflake under a microscope. It is certainly also true, as we shall see, that assumptions of symmetry have played a crucial and recently dominant role in theoretical physics. The question is whether the symmetry that delights us in our own experience and the symmetries that our physicists cite are sufficiently alike so that we can hope to attribute to the universe something close enough to the sensuous beauty symmetry gives us in our day-to-day lives.

We should start with a general definition of symmetry, a definition that technically fits both the cosmological and the ordinary examples. Symmetry means invariance under a stipulated transformation or substitution: something displays symmetry with respect to some transformation when that transformation leaves something unchanged. A sphere has full rotational symmetry in all dimensions: it looks the same in whichever of the three dimensions it is rotated. A square, in contrast, has ninety-degree symmetry in one dimension: it looks identical only when it is rotated by ninety degrees in a plane. A snowflake has hexagonal symmetry: it looks the same when rotated by sixty degrees. The Taj Mahal has ninety-degree rotational symmetry. Angelina Jolie's face has mirror-image symmetry: it looks the same in a mirror as full on.

These are all terrestrial symmetries. The symmetries that figure in physics are rather different. The most important may seem the most obvious. The basic laws of nature are invariant under any transformation of time, space, or orientation. An experiment confirms the same laws whether it is performed in Iceland or Chile or (so we assume) on an exoplanet three hundred million light-years away. Massachusetts has different laws from Rhode Island, but nature has different laws in no place. These we might call the background symmetries of physics. More specific symmetries might seem more dramatic. Einstein showed, in his special theory of relativity, that the same laws apply for two experimenters each moving at a different but constant velocity: light travels at the same speed as seen by each. In his general theory, he showed that laws are constant for two experimenters moving not only at different velocities but at different rates of acceleration: light still travels at the same speed for each of them. David Gross, a Nobel laureate, wrote that "Einstein's great advance in 1905 was to put symmetry first, to regard the symmetry principle as the primary feature of nature that constrains the allowable dynamical laws."[9] The success of the standard model lies essentially in the symmetries it displays in its fundamental equations of particles and forces.

Brian Greene spoke for the profession:

Physicists also believe [their] ... theories are on the right track because, in some hard-to-describe way, they *feel* right, and ideas of symmetry are essential to this feeling. ... the theories of the three forces other than gravity—electromagnetism and the strong and weak nuclear forces—are founded on other, somewhat more abstract but equally compelling principles of symmetry. So the symmetries of nature are not merely consequences of nature's laws. From our modern perspective, symmetries are the foundation from which laws spring.[10]

Our question, however, is not whether symmetry is crucial to the scientific search for a "final" theory, but whether symmetry explains the further presumption that the final theory will reveal resplendent beauty. The physicists seem to think so. They might be drawn to that merger of art and science, I suggested, by the fact that terrestrial symmetry is so often pleasing to our eyes: we tend to admire the symmetry of buildings and faces, and we are often disturbed by asymmetries. But the direct identification of cosmic beauty with cosmic symmetry nevertheless seems too crude. I agree that the symmetries of the universe seem so dramatically impressive, even as so far discovered, that they must have some important role to play in the assumption of final cosmic beauty I described. But we need a still deeper explanation of why they do.

Why too crude? First, symmetry is not so necessarily pleasing in our ordinary lives as the identification assumes. It is mirror image and rotational symmetry that we find most pleasing, but these symmetries often mean boredom rather than beauty. A desert without dunes and shadows would have complete rotational symmetry in our dimension of sight; it would look the same wherever we turned. But it would be boring, while a desert with random dunes, and therefore shadows, is gorgeous.

We must beware, moreover, of an important ambiguity in the terrestrial idea of symmetry. Sometimes, when we praise symmetry, we do not have any form of invariance in mind. We say that a painting or a sonnet achieves symmetry when its components are balanced in a satisfying way, even though they have no rotational or any other kind of technical symmetry at all. *The New American Dictionary* describes this usage as "special"; it defines it as "a pleasing proportion of the parts of a thing." A striking asymmetrical building may be symmetrical in that sense: Richard Rogers's Lloyd's Building in London, for instance, or Rem Koolhaas's Television Building in Beijing. But mere balance in art is not necessarily pleasing either: it may be mechanical. Whether symmetry in either sense makes for beauty is a complex matter sensitive to many factors. Also, symmetry lies rather near the sensuous pole of terrestrial beauty: we find it pleasing to the eye. The laws of physics that exhibit symmetries, on the contrary, lie at the purely intellectual end; if they give the universe beauty, this must be purely intellectual beauty. It must be the beauty of the equations and laws that explain these symmetries—the kind of pure intellectual beauty an elegant mathematical proof has, for example. But symmetry plays no conspicuous role in intellectual beauty. We do not count a mathematical proof or a legal argument more beautiful if it employs palindromes.

In any case, certainly from our selfish perspective, the asymmetries physicists describe are at least as important as the symmetries. Though the universe is symmetrical in a great variety of dimensions, it is not symmetrical in time: the future is different from the past everywhere. Every particle in the universe has a matching antiparticle; when these combine, they annihilate one another. Luckily there are more particles than antiparticles: if their numbers were symmetrical, nothing could exist. Some of the most impressive symmetries physicists have discovered are those that actually existed only for an incredibly short time after the birth of the universe and that can be recreated now only in unworldly gigantic particle accelerators. Everything that happened since—the formation of the elements, for instance— happened because the symmetries were immediately broken. The initial symmetries are of enormous theoretical importance. But can we think the universe beautiful because of what it so briefly was? Yes, we must recognize symmetry as in some deep way important to celestial beauty: we must take account of what, as Greene put it, "feels right" to physicists. But we need to probe deeper to explain that faith.

Is There a Way the Universe Just Is?

Here is an ancient philosophical problem. Is there a way the universe just is? Not for any reason but just because that is the way it happens to be? Will theoretical physics one day hit a wall that means there is just nothing more for it to learn? Will it end just in pointing a finger at what just happens to be?

The philosopher Gottfried Leibniz thought that a just-happens-to-be solution like that makes no sense. Nothing happens, he said, unless there is a "sufficient reason" for its happening. God made the universe and so it is a sufficient reason for the universe being the way it is that God wanted it that way. (Leibniz concluded that our world is therefore the best of all possible worlds because God could have no reason not to make it as good as possible. That is the view Voltaire ridiculed in his play *Candide;* he invented the sappy Dr. Pangloss as a disciple of Leibniz.) Still, it has seemed plausible to some great philosophers and physicists that the world just is, inexplicably, the way it is, so that science can only, finally, point its finger. Bertrand Russell declared that "the universe is just there, and that's all."[11] Richard Feynman, who is often called the most important physicist since Einstein, said that he could hope to explain how things work but not why they work that way. We must just accept, he said, "Nature as She is—absurd."[12]

Common sense agrees with Leibniz. It seems natural to think that, however the universe is configured, there must be some explanation why it is configured that way. If Einstein's theory can't account for how things were at the Big Bang, there must be a better explanation that can. We can't just say the theory doesn't apply to very small things and leave it at that. Theists, of course, believe there is an explanation of everything: Leibniz's explanation. The universe is the way it is because God made it that way. But if atheists think the universe is what it is, with no further explanation of why it is that way, they must think, like Russell, that the universe is just an eternal, inexplicable cosmic accident. That seems deeply unsatisfying.

True, in some contexts we must and do accept reason-ending answers. If you ask me why I like almonds, I can sensibly reply: "I just do." I would not deny that there is somewhere a further answer—in genetics or psychology, perhaps—though I can't imagine what it would be. But that is not the kind of answer you ask to have: you want a motivational answer and, within that domain, I can have nothing to say. I can't even explain why I have nothing to say. Motivational explanation just ends someplace, and here, for me, is where it ends. Physics, however, is meant to be the end of the explanatory road altogether. If there is no explanation of the birth and history of the universe there, there is no explanation anywhere.

Of course, an explanation of natural phenomena can rest on chance and probability: quantum mechanics, on at least some interpretations, holds that the behavior of particles is entirely indeterminate—they disappear and reappear in entirely unpredictable ways and places. But quantum theorists have made their theories plausible by showing how probabilities guarantee the firm predictabilities we encounter in the visible world: indeterminacy figures in explanation in that way. But why are the probabilities what they are? Quantum theory so far provides no answer, and if the accident hypothesis—that the universe just is a certain way—is right, there may be no answer to provide. We might, after all, have to say that the cookie just crumbled that way.

Still, that does seem deeply unsatisfactory. For one thing, scientists could never have any reason at all to suppose, at any point in the eons of physics to come, that they had actually reached the stopping point, that they were finally up against a wall of weirdness. They could never have any reason for rejecting the possibility—indeed probability—that they had not yet come upon some new mathematics or conceptual rearrangement or invention that would break through their stalemate. But that means that they could never have a reason even for thinking that the universe just is some way or other. Even if it is true that the universe just is some way or other, no one could have any reason to believe that.

From the perspective of a religious atheist, moreover, there is a further, even graver ground of dissatisfaction. If the universe just is whatever way it is, for no reason, then it would make no sense to presume that it is beautiful or awe-inspiring. It could then be beautiful, if at all, only by coincidence. Worse, because we could have no way of knowing how it just is, we could have no way of telling whether, as a matter of coincidence, it is in fact beautiful.

Are we therefore driven to the opposite answer to the ancient philosophical puzzle? Must we say that there is no end to explanation of the universe we inhabit, no "final" theory at all? That explanation can only go on, in an infinite regress, forever, so that we cannot even conceive of a stopping point being reached? That seems at least equally unsatisfactory. Our scientists could never have any reason to believe that either. How could they know that a truly final theory was not just around the corner?

There is an even more basic difficulty: if there is an infinite regress of explanation, then we are never justified in being fully confident about anything. For a further, deeper, explanation might show some fundamental assumption not to be true, at least in a way that justifies the inferences we draw from it.

In any case, this alternative answer would also be disobliging to an atheist's religious faith in the beauty of the universe. And for much the same reason. The presumption of beauty is a presumption about how things really are: the religious faith holds that the universe really is, at bottom, in the final explanation of everything, beautiful. But that presumption makes no sense if there is no bottom, no final explanation. If we must accept an infinite regress of explanation, beauty can be no more than skin deep.

Inevitability and the Universe

If we settle for either of the two most straightforward answers to our philosophical question, then we must give up the popular presumption I mentioned: that the universe is finally comprehensible through some all-encompassing theory. We do not comprehend the universe if we declare its enormous vastness and complexity just an accident we cannot explain or a puzzle whose unraveling must go on forever. There is, however, a third possibility. Let the physicist George Musser describe it.

> [Physicists] seek to boil the entire physical world down to equations compact enough to silk-screen onto a t-shirt that all the cool kids would wear. Actually, though, physicists' sartorial ambitions are more modest; they hope to create a theory that won't even need a shirt to write it on because it's so blindingly obvious.... They'll find that things are as they are because there's no other way they could be.... It's hard to create a consistent theory in any branch of physics because beautiful hypotheses have a nasty habit of collapsing under the weight of their own internal contradictions. In fact, physicists take

perverse pleasure from the fact that a quantum theory of gravity is taking so long to figure out. When they do figure it out, they'll have some confidence it must be right because there probably won't be any alternative.[13]

Einstein took the same view. Though he didn't believe in a god, he liked to invoke God metaphorically, as people often do, as a way of describing ultimate truth. When he was first told of the uncertainty principle of quantum mechanics, he said it couldn't be right because "God doesn't play dice with the universe." The truth about the structure of the entire universe, he thought, couldn't be an accident. It had to be a necessary truth. Perhaps not, as Musser put it, "blindingly obvious." But still inescapable.

This seems mysterious. How could the universe *necessarily* or *inevitably* just be a certain way? That is a far stronger claim than the much more familiar idea of physical and mental determinism. This holds that the future is entirely determined by the past: given what the laws of nature are and the way the world was at any particular time in the past, it is entirely fixed what will happen in the future. For most people, the most frightening consequence of determinism, so understood, is that human beings lack free will: our sense that we can decide what to do is an illusion because what we will do is determined by laws of nature operating on our brains. The claim of inevitability goes much further: it insists that it is inevitable not only what follows from laws of nature given a particular past, but what the laws of nature and the original starting point must be and have been.

What could justify or even give sense to such a strong claim? Imagine a "final" theory that sets out comprehensive laws explaining how the universe began and how it now is in its whole and in every part, laws that fit all current and predict all future observations. Suppose further that that theory could not be changed in any particular without destroying its explanatory power altogether: suppose, for instance, that any change would make the theory self-contradictory.

Weinberg sets out that requirement as a condition for the final theory he has in mind.

> Once you know the general physical principles adopted by Einstein, you understand that there is no other significantly different theory of gravitation to which Einstein could have been led. As Einstein said of general relativity, "The chief attraction of the theory lies in its logical completeness. If a single one of the conclusions drawn from it proves wrong, it must be given up; to modify it without destroying the whole structure seems to be impossible."[14]

Let us say that a theory of that character displays "strong integrity." Alas, strong integrity does not, on its own, solve the philosophical puzzle I described, for we can sensibly ask, even about a theory that meets those conditions, whether it just happens that the theory that fits and predicts all observations has strong integrity, or whether some prior explanation can be found showing why it has. But now we add a second requirement: the theory we imagine must *shield* its strong integrity in some way: by providing reasons *that emerge from the theory itself* showing that the idea of prior explanation cannot arise because it makes no sense.

Inevitability in science, I suggest, means shielded strong integrity. I shall offer examples of attempts to secure shielded integrity in contemporary physics. But we should first notice that the science part of familiar theistic religions is designed to satisfy exactly those conditions of shielded integrity. It is a familiar argument, across all the traditional godly religions, that the complexity of our world, and particularly the extraordinary complexity of human life, can be explained fully but only by supposing creation by a supernatural, omniscient, and all-powerful intelligence. Once this is accepted, everything we do or can observe is explained by that creation: it is shown to be inevitable given that supernatural power's imputed intentions. Leibniz's account is a straightforward example. But the philosophical puzzle is not yet answered. For what explains the existence of such an intelligence? Is it only an accident? If so, then the existence of everything is only a laughable coincidence. Does something, on the contrary, explain why God exists? But then the infinite regress is launched. The science of godly religion must shield itself from those questions.

From Plato on, but most explicitly in Aristotle's *Physics* and *Metaphysics,* the shield was thought to be supplied by the philosophical dilemma itself. Because everything that has a cause exists for a reason, and because an infinite regress is impossible, there must be an uncaused cause, a First Mover, a god. In medieval philosophy the logic became more complex. St Anselm developed one form of the ontological argument: because the very idea of god supposes his existence, and because we can comprehend that idea, god must exist. God, that is, is a conceptual necessity, which means that it makes no sense to suppose either that his existence is an accident or that it demands a causal explanation. There are other forms of the argument. Because God is eternal, for example, he is out of time altogether and we cannot conceive either of accident or causation except within way the necessity of mathematics is shielded. I have made the same claim of shielded integrity for the realm of value: that claim is part of my account of ungrounded value realism. A sound system of moral conviction has strong integrity—a coherence in which each judgment of personal or political morality supports the others—and that integrity is shielded, as in the case of mathematics, by the conceptual truth that nothing but another value judgment can support a judgment of value.[15]

We can easily understand why mathematics and value are immune from questions about their birth or causal provenance. But the edges of physics are still part of physics, so there is no domain insulation there. The cosmology must produce its own insulation, from within the domain, and so we must return to physics. Strong integrity is a familiar demand among physicists; I quoted Einstein's, Weinberg's, and Musser's formulations of the demand. If a successful theory of quantum gravity were to be found, it would unite the equations of gravity and those of the standard model by providing a more comprehensive theory from which they both flow. That would dramatically improve the integration of physics: it would mean that none of those equations could be altered without terminal damage to the theory as a whole: without in effect requiring an entirely new theory. When it was recently and briefly thought that neutrinos might travel faster than the speed of light, the feared consequences for cosmology and particle physics were not marginal but seismic.

Symmetries of some kind are essential for strong integration. There could be no strongly integrated theory of everything if we could not sensibly presume that the laws that govern local phenomena remain in force, and that the relative weights of electrons and protons do not shift, at observationally remote distances of space or time. Physicists significantly improved the integrity of their theories when they replaced their zoo of particles with quarks. A long list of particles and their effects could be altered in many respects with no effects on the rest; the types and laws of quarks create a stronger integrity. Integrity was dramatically further strengthened by the discovery that apparently thing else, more fundamental, explain the vibrating strings? If so, what explains that?

Science still needs a shield and, like theology, seeks one in the realm of concepts. (Secular science has become, in this respect, amazingly like the science of theology.) It was at least for some time common among cosmologists to insist that the Big Bang is the very origin of space and time, so that it makes no sense to ask why or where or what happened just before it occurred. Those of us who asked those questions were told that they were as silly as asking what is north of the North Pole. We can say how old the universe is—apparently about 14 billion years—because time itself is that old, but we cannot say, for example, for how long it didn't exist. If so, then on this thesis it makes no sense to ask for an explanation of why it occurred: explanations of physical phenomena presuppose causation, and causation requires space and time in which to operate. So explanation must, perforce, stop with a description of the Big Bang and a tracing forward of its inevitable consequences. There is no infinite regress because there is no regress at all. Nor need we declare the universe an untidy accident. True, we cannot offer a reason why it houses the laws it in fact does. But something is an accident only if it might well have been different, and we cannot say even that of the Big Bang. We would need a sense of the situation from which it emerged to call it an accident or to make any other judgment of probability. We cannot say even that it emerged, let alone that we have a sense of how.

This now perhaps passé story illustrates the requirement that, to be effective, a shield must be drawn from the theory it shields, not pasted on afterward. The nerve of that story is that time and law themselves begin only with the Big Bang, and that therefore nothing at all can be said about the circumstances of that event. But in recent years a more encompassing cosmology has been suggested and to some extent explored. This holds that our universe is not unique but is rather part of a "multiverse" of innumerably or perhaps infinitely many universes, a fantastically gigantic "anthropic" principle, is often used to ground an argument for the existence of a god. It could not be just an accident that the universe is so carefully tuned for life. The odds are too great against that result. There must be an explanation, and the only conceivable explanation is divine creation. The multiverse hypothesis purports to answer that argument. It is not an accident that our universe is carefully adjusted to make life possible, but neither do we need a creator god to explain the anthropic principle. If there are fabulously many universes constantly being born and dying, it is inevitable that at least one universe would be governed by exactly the laws of nature that govern ours. The odds are too great against there *not* being at least one such universe.

Is it then an accident that life happens to have landed on the one universe among those billions fit for life? No, of course not. Where else could it land? But why can't we still ask why there is a gigantic landscape from which universes bubble up? Is that just an accident? Or can we find a reason why that should exist? Once again the hypothesis of distinct universes might be thought to supply a shield. We stop the regress by pointing out, again, that though we might have an argument that other universes exist, we are conceptually barred from asking what causes the phenomenon of their birth and death because even if there are hosts of other universes, our concept of causation is formed out of the laws of our own universe and cannot be exported in that way. These various conceptual shields do not exhaust the possibilities, and, as I said, we do not yet have a fully integrated theory to shield. But they nevertheless all illustrate the condition our account of inevitability imposes. They all arise out of the theory they are designed to shield; they are not imposed on that theory as dei ex machina.

The Beauty of Inevitability

A comprehensive "final" theory would show the inevitability of the laws of nature in the greatest possible scope and detail—inevitability in the only sense in which the pertinent logic of explanation permits. If that understanding of a final theory is roughly right, it supplies a solution to the first of our simultaneous equations. It ties the physicists' reigning presumption that the universe is comprehensible to a possible candidate for the kind of beauty so many of them claim for that universe. They sense beauty in the fact—if it is a fact—that the laws that govern everything there is in the vastness of space and in the minutiae of existence are so delicately interwoven that each is explicable only through the others, so that nothing could be different without there being nothing.

But now we confront the second challenge. Is this really beauty? It would after all be possible to survey this inevitability with no passion at all: simply to count it as only a value-neutral property of the gas and energy. That is presumably the reaction of the skeptical naturalists I described in Chapter 1. They might perhaps say that they find the idea of inevitability exciting or pleasing. Or that they have an emotional reaction to that idea rather like the reaction they have to symmetrical architecture or pretty sunsets. I ask, however, about something very different: the wonder of scientists who think that the beauty they sense in the cosmos is as real as electrons and headaches and galaxies. We can sustain that thought only by making sense of inevitability as an aspect or dimension of real beauty more generally, across the spectrum of terrestrial beauty I described.

Once we look for inevitability there, however, we find it very quickly. It is part—though only part—of what we admire in great creative work that given its boundaries every part seems essential to the others, its beginnings can be read from its endings, its top from its bottom, its middle from those boundaries. It is, in the term I proposed for physics, fully integrated. Its boundaries, moreover, are not arbitrary: as in physics they are dictated from within. The novel creates its own beginning and end: we might ask why it begins where it does, but only as a question to be answered from within its own four corners, by seeing its beginning as a literary decision, sensitive to whatever theory we have about what frames its value as art. In art as in cosmology we need a theory—in art it is a theory of the value of art—to stipulate the limits of pertinent analysis or explanation and so to shield the integrity we seek. I need examples to rescue these abstractions, but I must first make necessary qualifications explicit. The integrity I am trying to describe is obviously not sufficient to make great or even decent art: it is only one dimension that contributes to the value of art. Nor is integrity even necessary to art: some art not only does not aim at integrity but aims to defeat it: happenings, atonal music, action painting, and stream-of-consciousness fiction, for example.

We might take our first example from Weinberg's own comparison of physics and art. "In Raphael's *Holy Family*," he writes, "the placement of every figure on the canvas is perfect. This may not be of all paintings in the world your favorite, but as you look at that painting, there is nothing that you would want Raphael to have done differently."[16] This might be a slight exaggeration, but only slight. We are drawn to this idea of inevitability, certainly as a first impression, in so many of the greatest works. We feel that nothing could be changed without catastrophe; the collapse of beauty into the mundane, the essential into an accident. When Emperor Joseph told Mozart that his *Figaro* had too many notes, Mozart replied, bewildered, that it has just enough. And so it does. Even the most surprising lines of poetry—about dolphin-torn or gong-tormented seas—suddenly seem, even in their mystery, inevitable. We feel the demands of tonal music viscerally: we yearn for resolutions, and when they come we can imagine no other way to resolve what had come before. We realize, in our hearing, that the brilliant chord was inevitable.

Henry James puts the point from the artist's perspective in his—characteristically difficult—preface to *The Ambassadors.*

> For the dramatist always, by the very law of his genius, believes not only in a possible right issue from the rightly-conceived tight

place; he does much more than this—he believes, irresistibly, in the necessary, the precious "tightness" of the place (whatever the issue) on the strength of any respectable hint. It being thus the respectable hint that I had with such avidity picked up, what would be the story to which it would most inevitably form the centre? It is part of the charm attendant on such questions that the "story," with the omens true, as I say, puts on from this stage the authenticity of concrete existence. It then is, essentially—it begins to be, though it may more or less obscurely lurk, so that the point is not in the least what to make of it, but only, very delightfully and very damnably, where to put one's hand on it.[17]

The structural weaponry of art—genre, harmony, rhyme, meter, and the rest—all contribute to this sense of inevitability, and may owe their history and their force to our craving for it. Our knowledge of the sonnet form contributes hugely to our sense, in retrospect, of the inevitability of any good sonnet's resolution. Our delight in Cole Porter's internal rhymes, if less profound, has the same basis. I must be careful not to overstate this point. I do not mean that great art is strongly integrated in all detail, but rather that the level of its integration contributes to its greatness. No doubt lines of *Macbeth* could be changed—indeed have been changed in various editions—without damaging the play. But the greatness of the play rests in good part on the integrity of the images it provides, most of which contribute not just to the play's overall force but also to the individual strength of other images, and—principally—by the building sense that the tragedy must end as it does. It is not just art in the conventional sense in which integrity and inevitability play their role: they contribute almost across the whole spectrum I described from nearly entirely sensuous to purely intellectual. A mathematical proof or legal argument, as much as a poem or a play, becomes more beautiful as unnecessary lines or assumptions

by law and are necessary in a democratic society in the interests of public safety, for the protection of public order, health or morals, or for the protection of the rights and freedoms of others."[2] The First Amendment to the US Constitution prohibits government from either establishing a religion or restricting the free exercise of religion.

These various provisions are understood to have dramatic political consequences. They unambiguously prohibit government from penalizing membership in any conventional religion or membership in none. They are often, though not universally, understood also to forbid government to declare any religion an official state religion, or to support one religion or all religions through subsidies or other special privileges, or to permit legal constraints of any sort that assume that one religion is preferable to others or that religion is preferable to none. It makes a considerable practical difference what counts as a religion for purposes of these provisions. Is religion limited, for these documents, to opinions about the existence or nature of a god? Or does religion include all religious convictions including those that, if I am right, an atheist may hold? If free exercise of religion is limited to the practice or denial of theism, then it would not protect abortion rights, for instance. True, much of the opposition to abortion assumes that a god has forbidden that act. But not all opposition is based on theism, and few women who want an abortion believe that a god has ordered them to abort. If, on the contrary, freedom of religion is not restricted to opinions about a god, but embraces all deep convictions about the purpose and responsibilities of life, then it might be thought an open question whether the right to abortion is a religious issue.

References to "religion" in constitutional documents are understood by most people, I believe, as pointing to institutionally organized churches or other groups worshipping some form of god, or something, like a Buddha, close to a god. Certainly the original battles for religious freedom were fought to secure freedom to choose which such group to join in heart and practice. John Locke, one of the earliest champions of religious freedom, was careful to exclude atheists from its protection: atheists, he said, should not be allowed rights of citizens.[3] Later, however, the right to religious freedom became understood to include freedom not only to choose among theist religions but to choose no such religion: atheists fell under its protection. But the right was still understood as the right to make one's own choice about the existence and nature of a god. I will soon describe decisions by the Supreme Court and other courts that extended the protection to groups that did regard themselves as religions without god—the Ethical Culture society in the United States, for example. But historically, and for most people still, a religion means a belief in some form of god. Should this fact of common understanding be decisive in determining who is entitled to the protection the various documents declare?

No, because the interpretation of basic constitutional concepts does not depend on common understandings or dictionary definitions. They are interpretive concepts whose use demands a very different kind of test. Such interpretive concepts—liberty, equality, dignity, religion, and the rest—form the nerve of political ideals. We use them to decide what to protect as human and constitutional rights, and we must define them so as to make sense of that crucial role. How must we understand the concept of religion if we are to justify the assumption that freedom of religion is an important basic right? How must religion be conceived if people are to have a protected freedom for their religious choices and activities that they do not enjoy in other aspects of their lives? We must reject any account of the nature or scope of religion that would make a distinct right to religious freedom silly or arbitrary. I have argued so far that we best account for the variety and importance of people's convictions by adopting a conception of religion that is deeper than theism. Now we look at the question differently: as a matter of political morality as well as philosophical depth.

Is Religious Freedom Only about God?

Can we find a persuasive reason why the freedom of religion should extend to the choice among godly religions, including a choice to reject them all, but no further? Here is one suggestion: The history of religious war and persecution shows that the choice of which gods to worship is a matter of special, transcendental importance to billions of people. Such people have shown themselves willing to kill others who worship different gods or the same gods in different ways, and also to be killed rather than abandon their own way of worshipping their own gods. That passion was the cause of the terrible religious wars in Europe that made religious toleration imperative there. It continues to spawn mass murder in our time in the Middle East and elsewhere. No other issue arouses that intensity of emotion, and the world has had and continues to have that reason for guaranteeing religious freedom in political constitutions and international conventions.

These striking facts certainly help to explain the birth of the idea of religious freedom and its rapid growth in popularity: why people in seventeenth-century Europe, for instance, sensed its pressing importance in securing peace. But they do not explain why a special right is needed to protect only godly religions now in the large parts of the world, including the United States and Europe, where violent religious wars are anyway not in the cards. The sects that benefit from freedom of religion in those countries are unpopular minority faiths whose members could not produce effective rebellion if their freedom were denied. In any case, moreover, religious freedom is very widely regarded as a human right, not just a useful legal construction, and policy arguments about the need for peace are inadequate to justify a basic right. We need a different kind of argument to defend a conception of religious freedom. We need to identify some particularly important interest people have, an interest so important that it deserves special protection against official or other injury. So our immediate question must be: Can we identify any special interest that people have because they believe in a god that they would not have if, like Einstein and millions of others, they subscribe to a religion without god?

The science of many theistic religions declares that a god can and will destroy populations or send people to a hell in anger at their disobedience. That divine power was once widely thought to argue for forcing people to worship in a particular sect. It hardly argues for a freedom that permits people to worship in ways that will make such a god angry. Suppose we say, then, that people who fear damnation live in a kind of terror that atheists do not, and that they require a special protection on that account? So explained, the right is over-inclusive because many people who belong to orthodox religions do not believe in an afterlife of reward or punishment. It is also over-inclusive in a different way: it protects atheists from prosecution, and tolerating atheists can lead only to a god's anger. In any case, people have many fears. Some tremble at the possibility that a new particle accelerator will destroy the planet.

However, these considerations do not justify a freedom that is limited to the exercise of orthodox, godly religions, because atheists often have convictions of duty that are for them equally imperative. Pacifism is a familiar example: the US Supreme Court properly interpreted a statute providing conscientious objection for those whose religious beliefs forbid killing to include an atheist with the same convictions. In Chapter 1 I described a more abstract conviction that I count as a matter of religious faith: that each person has an intrinsic and inescapable ethical responsibility to make a success of his life. That responsibility is part of the religious attitude that both believers and atheists can share. It includes a responsibility of each person to decide for himself ethical questions about which kinds of lives are appropriate and which would be degrading for him. A state violates that right whenever it prohibits or burdens homosexual practice, for instance. So this justification of religious freedom—that self-respect needs special protection—provides no ground for limiting that freedom to the orthodox religions of believers.

In the United States, the establishment clause of the First Amendment prohibits government from designating one religion or sect as the official faith of the country, as the Church of England is the official faith of Great Britain. But the establishment clause has been understood to prohibit much more than that: it has been understood to ban prayer in public schools, crèches at Christmas on public squares, replicas of the Ten Commandments on courthouse walls, and the teaching of allegedly faith-based science in state schools. These banned displays and practices are all regarded as ways in which government takes sides, or at least might be seen as taking sides, among religions or between believers and atheists. But is there any reason it should be thought wrong to take sides between orthodox theistic religions, but not to take sides between alternate views of what counts as living well? Not wrong to take sides, for instance, between alternate views of healthy sexuality?

It is sometimes said that when government takes sides among religions—for example by declaring Calvinism the official faith of the nation—it declares that those who worship a god in some other way, or who worship no god at all, count as less than full citizens. So providing a period for prayer in state schools, or teaching that the creation of the universe is the work of an intelligent designer, offers less than equal respect to those who have no god to pray to or to credit with creation. It uses state or national funds, collected in taxes in part from them, to affirm a national identity that excludes them. But now consider the position of a homosexual in a state that praises and protects the institution of marriage in a variety of ways, and provides arrangements and officials to marry men and women, but excludes homosexuals from marriage. Or, for that matter, consider a committed monarchist who is surrounded by official declarations of the nation's commitment to democracy. I do not mean to suggest—I will very soon deny—that religious freedom grants monarchists immunity from public endorsement of democracy. I mean only that we cannot deny them that immunity just because they do not draw their opinion from some conception of a god.

Freedom Out of Control?

We have not discovered a justification for offering religion a right to special protection that is exclusive to theistic religions. So we must expand that right's scope to reflect a better justification. How? The answer might seem obvious: we must just declare that people have a right in principle to the free exercise of their profound convictions about life and its responsibilities, whether derived from a belief in god or not, and that government must stand neutral in policy and expenditure toward all such convictions. That would simply extrapolate the special rights and privileges now restricted to conventional religion to all passionately held conviction. But no community could possibly accept that extended right.

Consider those many people who in the popular phrase "worship" Mammon. They subscribe, perhaps passionately, to the conviction that a successful life is one full of material success. They treat this goal as one of transcendent importance. They are wracked with remorse at bad investments or missed financial opportunities. But we cannot think that religious freedom for such people therefore includes exempting them from income tax. Consider racists who think that racial integration corrupts and destroys the purity of their and their children's lives. Their aversions, they say, are not matters of taste but reflect a view about the responsibilities of people to live with their own kind. We cannot think that government law and policy must show neutrality toward that view. If we decided that all religious attitudes are entitled to special protection, we would need a more restrictive definition of a religious attitude than I have so far provided.

We might consider two kinds of stricter definition: a functional definition that fixes on the role of the putative conviction in a person's overall personality or a substantive definition that designates only certain convictions about how to live as deserving constitutional protection. The US Supreme Court provided a functional definition in response to Daniel Andrew Seeger's claim that he was entitled to conscientious-objector status in the Vietnam War even though he was an atheist. He relied on the following language in the statute authorizing the draft.

> Nothing contained in this title shall be construed to require any person to be subject to combatant training and service in the armed forces of the United States who, by reason of religious training and belief, is conscientiously opposed to participation in war in any form. Religious training and belief in this connection means an individual's belief in a relation to a Supreme Being involving duties superior to those arising from any human relation, but does not include essentially political, sociological, or philosophical views or a merely personal moral code.[4]

In spite of the statute's reference to "a Supreme Being," the Supreme Court upheld Seeger's claim. It assumed that Congress would not have wanted to discriminate among religious convictions, and offered this account of what these are:

> The test might be stated in these words: A sincere and meaningful belief which occupies in the life of its possessor a place parallel to that filled by the God of those admittedly qualifying for the exemption comes within the statutory definition.[5]

It is difficult to parse this requirement, however. In what way is a belief that war is wrong "parallel" to a belief in God? However we answer that question, we might worry that a serious worshipper of Mammon meets the test.

A substantive definition that restricts the range of passionate convictions that a right to religious freedom should protect seems more appropriate. This identifies religious convictions that qualify for protection through their subject matter, not the fervor with which they are held. In 1992 I tried to provide a substantive definition as part of an argument for a First

Amendment approach to the abortion question. I said, "Religions attempt to answer the deeper existential question by connecting individual human lives to a transcendent objective value."[6] I quoted a statement of an Ecumenical Council: "Men expect from the various religions answers to the riddles of the human condition: What is man? What is the meaning and purpose of our lives?"[7] I said that the question whether the US Constitution protects a woman's right to an early abortion is therefore a question about the reach of its First Amendment's religion clauses. "I can think of no plausible account of the content a belief must have, in order to be religious in character," I said, "that would rule out convictions about why and how human life has intrinsic objective importance."[8]

In their opinions in a Supreme Court decision confirming that women have a constitutional right to an early abortion, three justices offered a similar substantive account of choices they said the Constitution protects:

Matters, involving the most intimate and personal choices a person may make in a lifetime, choices central to personal dignity and autonomy, are central to the liberty protected by the Fourteenth Amendment. At the heart of liberty is the right to define one's own concept of existence, of meaning, of the universe, and of the mystery of human life.[9]

Other judges and courts have emphasized a further limitation: that a religious conviction must be part of and drawn from a general, sincere, coherent, integrated, and comprehensive account of why it is important for people to live well and what it is to live well.[10] People who hold a religious conviction according to that heightened standard need not be able to identify that larger, more comprehensive view in any articulate or self-conscious way. It is rather a matter of interpretation whether the explicit convictions for which someone seeks protection fit sufficiently comfortably into some recognizable comprehensive view of that kind, and whether his life and other opinions are reasonably consistent with that more comprehensive view. Members of some established church fit the description unless their behavior shows only an insincere commitment to its tenets. But the description also comfortably embraces nontheistic convictions—about pacifism or the permissibility of abortion, for instance. In its *Torcaso* decision, the Supreme Court listed, among religions meeting the test it had in mind, humanist societies that are explicitly atheistic.[11]

These substantive restrictions on the convictions a right to religious freedom should protect are all appealing. But their plausibility relies on the assumption that it lies within the power of government to choose among sincere convictions to decide which are worthy of special protection and which not. That assumption seems itself to contradict the basic principle that questions of fundamental value are a matter of individual, not collective, choice. We cannot assume that the convictions government chooses not to protect are insincere or otherwise not genuine.

not to discriminate in favor of any religion over others. But an exemption for one faith from a constraint imposed on people of other faiths discriminates against those other faiths on religious grounds. American constitutional lawyers are well aware of this conflict. There are two "religion" clauses in the First Amendment: one prohibits government from infringing the "free exercise" of religion; the other prohibits it from "establishing" a religion—that is, giving a religion special official recognition or protection. The lawyers say that the first of these clauses often conflicts with the second.

The Native American Church uses peyote, a hallucinogenic drug, in its religious rituals. The drug is generally banned because it is dangerously addictive. If an exception is made for a tribe because the drug plays a role in its rituals, then the law discriminates on grounds of religion against, for instance, followers of Aldous Huxley who believe that the best life is lived in a trance. If the law therefore recognizes godless religion, and exempts everyone who thinks that hallucinogenic drugs allow special perception into the meaning of life, then the law discriminates, also on religious grounds, against those who only want to get high.[12]

Another example: the Catholic Church does not permit the many adoption agencies it operates to assign children to same-sex couples. The government refuses to fund agencies that adopt that policy. The Church insists that, because its tenets forbid same-sex unions, the government's policy discriminates against them on religious grounds.[13] The government replies that an exemption from its rules for the Church would discriminate in the Church's favor against other agencies that might have their own reasons, not grounded in theistic religion, for refusing adoption to same-sex couples.

Now consider a more complex and revealing example. The principle that government may not "establish" any religion means that the religious doctrine of one particular religion may not be taught in public schools as truth. But as I said in Chapter 1, each religion has a science department and so the question arises whether and how far its science may be taught, just as science, in public schools. This has become a particular problem for biology classes in the United States. A Pennsylvania school district ordered teachers to mention theories about the origin of life that reject Darwin's random-mutation theory of evolution and claim to provide evidence that human beings were created by a supernatural intelligence. A federal court judge declared the order unconstitutional under the "establishment" clause. He said that the school board's decision was based on religious conviction, not scientific judgment.

Thomas Nagel has provided an illuminating analysis of the issue.[14] He points out that someone's judgment on the question whether divine authorship or random mutation provides a better explanation of human life is crucially influenced by his prior beliefs about whether a god exists. An atheist will from the start rule out divine creation: even if the chances that random mutation and selection would produce human life are antecedently small, intelligent design is not an alternative. But a

right to what we might call "ethical independence"
and also special rights to particular liberties.[15]
The first of these components, ethical independence, means that government must never restrict
freedom just because it assumes that one way for
people to live their lives—one idea about what
lives are most worth living just in themselves—is
intrinsically better than another, not because its
consequences are better but because people who
live that way are better people. In a state that prizes
freedom, it must be left to individual citizens,
one by one, to decide such questions for themselves, not up to government to impose one view
on everyone. So government may not forbid drug
use just because it deems drug use shameful, for
example; it may not forbid logging just because it
thinks that people who do not value great forests
are despicable; it may not levy highly progressive
taxes just because it thinks that materialism is
evil. But of course ethical independence does not
prevent government from interfering with people's
chosen ways of life for other reasons: to protect
other people from harm, for example, or to protect

natural wonders, or to improve the general welfare. So it may forbid drugs to protect the community from the social costs of addiction, it may levy taxes to finance roads and aid the poor, and it may protect forests because forests are in fact wonderful. It may protect forests for that reason even though none of its citizens thinks a life wandering among them has any value.

Ethical independence, that is, stops government from restricting freedom only for certain reasons and not for others. Special rights, on the other hand, place much more powerful and general constraints on government. Freedom of speech is a special right: government may not infringe that special freedom unless it has what American lawyers have come to call a *"compelling"* justification. Speakers may not be censored even when what they say may well have bad consequences for other people: because they campaign for forest despoliation or because it would be expensive to protect them from an outraged crowd. The right to free speech can be abridged only in emergencies: only to prevent, again in a phrase beloved of American lawyers, a clear and present—and, we might add, grave—danger. The right to due process and a fair trial for those accused of crime is another special right; it raises even higher barriers. Government has no right to indict someone it thinks innocent, or to try anyone without the traditional protections of fair trials, even when it believes that security would be greatly improved if it did.

Now I can put a suggestion. The problems we encountered in defining freedom of religion flow from trying to retain that right as a special right while also decoupling religion from a god. We should consider, instead, abandoning the idea of a special right to religious freedom with its high hurdle of protection and therefore its compelling need for strict limits and careful definition. We should consider instead applying, to the traditional subject matter of that supposed right, only the more general right to ethical independence. The difference between these two approaches is important. A special right fixes attention on the subject matter in question: a special right of religion declares that government must not constrain religious exercise in any way, absent an extraordinary emergency. The general right to ethical independence, on the contrary, fixes on the relation between government and citizens: it limits the reasons government may offer for any constraint on a citizen's freedom at all.

We should ask: Are the convictions we want to protect sufficiently protected by the general right to ethical independence, so that we do not need a troublesome special right? If we decide they are, then we have strong grounds for a radical reinterpretation of all the constitutions, conventions, and human rights covenants. We must understand the moral right to religious freedom they declare as a right to ethical independence. We know why, historically, the right was expressed as limited to religion, but we insist that we make best contemporary sense of the right, and supply the best available justification for it, by taking religious tolerance as an example of the more general right.

So I repeat our question: Does the general right to ethical independence give us the protection that, on reflection, we believe we need? That general right protects the historical core of religious freedom. It condemns any explicit discrimination or establishment that assumes—as such discrimination invariably does assume—that one variety of religious faith is superior to others in truth or virtue or that a political majority is entitled to favor one faith over others or that atheism is father to immorality.[16] Ethical independence protects religious conviction in a more subtle way as well: by outlawing any constraint neutral on its face but whose design covertly assumes some direct or indirect subordination. Is that protection enough? Do we need a special right requiring not just a neutral but a compelling justification for any constraint?

Return to peyote and ritual. When the Supreme Court held that the First Amendment does not require an exemption for the Native American Church, Congress, outraged, passed the Religious Freedom Restoration Act,[17] which insisted that the Court's decision was wrong. Was Congress right? Not if we test the Court's decision against the general right of ethical independence.

The general right does not protect the religious use of a banned hallucinogenic drug when that use threatens general damage to the community. So Congress's statute reversing the Court's decision was, in effect, a declaration that religion needs more protection than general ethical independence offers. No regulation that interferes with a religious practice is permitted, Congress declared, however innocent and nondiscriminating its purpose, unless there is a "compelling" rather than simply an ordinary need for regulation—unless, that is, the regulation is necessary to prevent some emergency or grave danger. The Religious Freedom Restoration Act was wildly popular.[18] But the Court was right as a matter of political morality and Congress wrong. If the Native American Church is entitled to an exemption from drug-control laws, then Huxley followers would also be entitled to an exemption, and skeptical hippies would be entitled to denounce the entire drug-control regime as a religious establishment.

If we deny a special right to free exercise of religious practice, and rely only on the general right to does not deny equal concern. That priority of non-discriminatory collective government over private religious exercise seems inevitable and right.

The New Religious Wars

Early in this book I described a new forum of the ancient religious wars: politics. We may put our new hypothesis—that the general right to ethical independence gives religion all the protection appropriate—to a more concrete test by considering the heated controversies of those wars in its light. These are not battles between different organized religions; they are wars between the believers and nonbelievers. In many nations it is now a particularly divisive issue whether emblems of religious allegiance may be worn in public schools, governmental offices and buildings, and public space. There have been acrimonious and sometimes violent battles about whether public schools may set aside time for private silent prayer during a school day, whether the Ten

Commandments may be placed on a courthouse wall, whether a city or town may place a crèche on a public square at Christmas, whether headscarves or burkas may be prohibited in schools or on the streets, and whether minarets may be prohibited in Swiss cantons. Some of the practices on this list seem to raise what American lawyers call issues of free exercise and others what they call issues of religious establishment. But we may ask, of them all, how they must be resolved if the only pertinent political right is the general right of ethical independence.

Ethical independence does condemn official displays of the insignia of organized religions on courthouse walls or public streets unless these have genuinely been drained of all but ecumenical cultural significance—like city Santa Clauses visiting orphanages, for instance. Otherwise such displays use state funds or property to celebrate one godly religion, or godly religion in preference to godless religion or no religion. Headscarves and burkas are very different, however: these are private displays. What justification can a state provide for prohibiting anyone from wearing them anywhere?

It is sometimes said that a nation's law may properly aim to instill a sense of a shared secular identity of citizens that would be undermined by divisive badges of religious identification. But that assumes, in violation of the right of ethical independence, that one kind of identification is more admirable than another, or that, contrary to what many citizens think, religious identification is not sufficiently important to trump all patriotic identifications. A state may invent other justifications for such prohibitions that are not on their face violations of ethical independence. It may claim, for instance, that when some students wear badges of a particular religion, other students feel compelled to protest, out of a sense of duty to their own faith, and academic discipline and quality suffer. But there is no evidence for this and so it appears to be rationalization. Banning headscarves has long been a very divisive issue in Turkey; the long-standing ban has provoked rather than prevented much violence there.

Turkey is also the clearest example of why the ban offends ethical independence: it was a central part of Kemal Ataturk's campaign to change what Turks considered a responsible way to live their lives: to switch their culture from devout observance to full secularism.

Public school prayer is a more complex matter. Near one extreme is the British practice of requiring a daily Christian prayer in all except a few schools. Near the other is the French flat prohibition of any religious moment in public schools. In the United States, after an extended debate structured by several Supreme Court decisions, practice is apparently gravitating toward permitting schools to adopt what is called a "moment of silence" in which students are free to pray or, as it is frequently put, "meditate" as they wish. Or simply to rest their eyes. Ethical independence is, I think, satisfied by this practice unless the legislative record displays an intention specifically to benefit theistic religion. On its face, providing a moment of silence is neutral between godly and godless religious students and students who believe they have nothing to meditate about.

Now consider religion in public education from the perspective of the general right to ethical independence rather than a special right with respect to religion. I mentioned earlier a particular issue: Does a public school board violate religious freedom when it mandates the teaching of intelligent design in biology classes as an alternative to Darwinian evolution? Nagel, recall, pointed out that the assumption that intelligent design is bad science presupposes atheism, which is a religious position, so that banning intelligent design means the state taking sides on a religious matter. His point is pertinent when we understand religious freedom in subject-matter terms, as a special right requires. If we rely not on any special right, however, but on the more general right to ethical independence, we see the matter differently.

Ethical independence requires that government not restrict citizens' freedom when its justification assumes that one conception of how to live, of what makes a successful life, is superior to others. It is often an interpretive question, and sometimes a difficult one, whether a policy does reflect that assumption. In the circumstances of American culture, a school board's decision to mandate the teaching of intelligent design as an alternative to Darwinism reflects not only the assumption that a god capable of creation exists, just as a strict matter of cosmic history, but the endorsement of a full set of ethical attitudes about the role of religion in a well-lived life and an ambition to inculcate those ethical attitudes in new generations. It does not wish simply to restore balance to an academic subject, as a board might that insisted that American history include material documenting the abuses of slavery. The political campaigns that first tried to make schools teach creationism—that the Earth is only seven thousand years old—and then pressed the apparently more sophisticated intelligent design thesis when the courts ruled creationism out are different: they are part of a national campaign of the so-called religious right to increase the role of godly religion in public life. That is an interpretive judgment but not, I think, a difficult one. The American judge who declared unconstitutional a requirement to teach intelligent design in public schools relied on that interpretive conclusion. He held that the histories, practices, and statements of the majority members of the school board suggested that they were acting not primarily for purely academic motives but in the spirit of that national campaign.

The same interpretive question might be asked, of course, about a school board's decision to teach the evidence for and against Darwin's theory without mentioning the alternative of intelligent design. We might ask whether that decision reflects an ambition to persuade students away from theistic religion. That would be an implausible hypothesis in modern American culture, however. The scientific and lay communities that have accepted the general theme of Darwinian evolutionary theory include a great number of people who hold to some godly religion; they believe that their belief in evolution is perfectly consistent with a belief in a god. Nor can science teachers sensibly be understood as engaged in any campaign to promote atheism. When we judge the matter from the perspective of ethical independence, we find not Nagel's symmetry but an important asymmetry.

We come back, finally, to what is undoubtedly the most divisive issue of all: sexual and reproductive morality. When the Supreme Court decided that a state lacks power to criminalize homosexual acts, or early abortions, it located its opinions doctrinally in the equal protection and due process clauses of the US Constitution rather than the First Amendment's guarantees of religious freedom. It had no choice. Opponents of homosexuality and abortion very often cite a god's will as warrant, but not invariably, and, as I said, few men or women who want choice in these matters conceive their desire as grounded in religion. But if, quite apart from the state of American constitutional law, we treat religious freedom as part of ethical independence, then the liberal position becomes mandatory. So does gender equality in marriage. I have argued for these claims in other work, and though even this summary statement will provoke dismay, I will not repeat or elaborate on my arguments here.[19]

In 2009, in a referendum decision that shocked the world, Swiss citizens amended their constitution to prohibit the building of minarets anywhere in their country. The federal government and the Catholic Church, among a great variety of institutions, opposed the ban, but it nevertheless succeeded by a substantial majority in a referendum. One of the main proponents of the ban argued that because the Islamic religion does not require minarets to be built at mosques, the prohibition could not be regarded as a violation of freedom of religion. If we conceive freedom of religion as a special right confined to religious subjects, then the fact that minarets answer to no religious duty or requirement—if that is a fact—might seem pertinent. But if we conceive of religious freedom as a central case of a more general right to ethical independence, that fact becomes wholly irrelevant. No one familiar with the controversy can doubt that the referendum vote expressed an indiscriminate condemnation of the religion and culture of Islam. It declared war on the egalitarian ideal of ethical independence.

I close this chapter with a hope; indeed, if you won't object, a prayer. In this book I suggest that people share a fundamental religious impulse that has manifested itself in various convictions and emotions. For most of history, that impulse has generated two kinds of convictions: a belief in an intelligent supernatural force—a god—and a set of profound ethical and moral convictions. These two kinds of belief are both consequences of the more fundamental attitude, but they are independent of one another. Atheists can therefore accept theists as full partners in their deepest religious ambitions. Theists can accept that atheists have the same grounds for moral and political conviction as they do. Both parties may come to accept that what they now take to be a wholly unbridgeable gap is only an esoteric kind of scientific disagreement with no moral or political implications. Or at least many more of them can. Is that much too much to hope? Probably.

4

DEATH AND IMMORTALITY

I SHOULD SAY SOMETHING, though I will not say much, about death. When Woody Allen was told that he would live on in his work, he replied that he would rather live on in his apartment. Most godly religions hold out the hope of something that should seem even better than that: an eternal living on in the most unimaginably wonderful circumstances. Quite literally unimaginable. Great painters show good people rising filled with helium, and popular cartoonists draw quite ordinary people sitting on clouds or pleading before a white-bearded man with a key. Silly evasions like these are inevitable because the question of what life after death actually means cannot even begin to be answered. Nevertheless the bare offer undoubtedly enhances the appeal of those religions that make it. Life after death doesn't have to be imaginable—we don't have to decide what we will look like or whether we can see without eyes or move without limbs or what, if anything, we will remember—because the intense visceral appeal of the idea is entirely negative. Life after death actually only means something—anything—that is *not* what we desperately dread: the total, obliterating, itself unimaginable, snuffing out of everything.

But is a god really required to provide some kind of alternative—any kind of alternative—to total obliteration? A god is required if life after death is a miracle and only a god can make a miracle. But why couldn't some story different from oblivion be a natural fact, like the phenomena of quantum fluctuations that are now claimed to bring a universe out of nothing? Quantum theory is full of what might once have been thought miracles: a cat in a closed box, for instance, that is neither alive nor dead until the box is opened. We might try to imagine some mental stuff that is distinct to a particular human being, different for each, that is constantly emanated by his brain into space, and the sum of which, in countless independent quanta, survives the death of that brain. A bizarre but natural soul? What then? Perhaps reincarnation, which is favored in some religious traditions: the natural soul somehow re-unites in a different, nascent brain. Or perhaps it just perdures as independent quanta until the end of the universe. Or perhaps it survives even the death of the universe because it rides on the back of new universes emerging. These are fantastical, but physics has anyway become fantastical, on its own. Quantum behavior is not a miracle that re-quires a god, because it is not a violation of natu-ral law. On the contrary, our scientists struggle to find a natural law that fits. I agree that the pros-pect that one's natural soul survives one's death as quantum fragments is not in the least com-forting. But if all we really crave is not being turned into nothing, then this would at least secure that.

So life after death does not necessarily require miracles. The science of a godless religion may other people. It would be inconsistent with any purpose we can sensibly ascribe to the Sistine God (rather than the pagan gods) to suppose that he would be satisfied with obedience out of fear.

For a plausible answer we must reverse the order of inference that has long seemed natural. We have assumed that judgment is necessary because there exists a punitive god. We should rather think that a god is necessary because a god's existence makes judgment possible. We are conscious of our mortality in many ways, but for those with the religious attitude I described in Chapter 1, one of these ways is essentially judgmental. We think that, because we are mortal, it matters how we live; it matters, in the familiar diction, what someone does with his one life. We think of our life as a whole, as something we have made through our decisions and our fortunes, and we want that creation to be a good one. Not everyone takes this religious attitude, of course, at least consciously; indeed, many people say they are skeptical about the very idea that a life could be good or bad rather than simply long or short, pleasant or

standard of living well? In that case, the Sistine
God has only his own opinion about what that
standard holds. We might think we have good
reason to think that that god's opinion is very
likely to be better than our own. But what is in-
dispensable is not that judgment about moral
and ethical expertise but the necessarily prior
judgment that there is an objective ethical and
moral truth that someone might sensibly be
thought to be an expert about. And that prior
judgment does not depend on any theist assumption. It is as much available to an atheist as to a
theist. Provided, that is, that the atheist is a religious atheist.

That is the crucial point. What matters most
fundamentally to the drive to live well is the conviction that there is, independently and objectively, a right way to live. That is at the center of
what I described, in Chapter 1, as a religious attitude to life. It is not available to a naturalist who
thinks that reality consists only of matter and
mind: that values are either illusions or fictions
constructed out of matter and mind. In this most

fundamental respect religious theists and religious atheists are at one. The existence or nonexistence of a god does not figure in the instinct of value that unites them. What divides them is science: they disagree about the best explanation of the truths of matter and mind, but it by no means follows that they disagree about the further truths of value.

What should we count as immortality? The literal meaning supposes staying alive forever, perhaps on Olympus or even in an apartment. But nothing will give us that: not even the most beneficent Sistine God. Acolytes of that god do speak of life in the clouds, but we can make no real sense of that. It is just negation—we do not become nothing—and so it is not a theory of immortality but just leaves a place open for one. We just imagined one way to continue: we imagined quanta of mental stuff once part of you but now at liberty in the universe. We can stipulate that this, or something like it, counts as immortality. But why should we? Any plausible account of what we should deem immortality must make it something we should covet: something of value to us. Disassociated mental quanta do not make that grade.

Where else might we turn? Woody Allen's admirer might have had two different things in mind. He might have meant that, like Homer and Shakespeare, Allen would be celebrated for many centuries. But he might not be: good as Allen has been, he might be forgotten, as presumably have many comic geniuses much praised in their time. And eventually, of course, as species evolve or our planet burns, the reputations of even those giants will no longer exist. Or the admirer might have had something quite different in mind: not a prediction but an assessment. He might have meant that Allen's films constituted a timeless achievement that evolution, history, or fate cannot change: like other works of art they are an out-of-time achievement just in having been made, whether or not they continue to be admired or even survive.

We might think of a life that way. The Romantic poets said we should try to make our lives into works of art. Perhaps they thought only about artists or other people differently creative. But what they said can be applied to any life someone self-consciously leads supposing it to be a life lived well according to a plausible view of what that means. Someone creates a work of art from his life if he lives and loves well in family or community with no fame or artistic achievement at all.

> Does all that strike you as silly? Just sentimental? When you do something smaller well—play a tune or a part or a hand, throw a curve or a compliment, make a chair or a sonnet or love—your satisfaction is complete in itself. Those are achievements within life. Why can't a life also be an achievement complete in itself, with its own value in the art in living it displays?[1]

If we do crave that kind of achievement, as I believe we should, then we could treat it as a kind of immortality. We face death believing we have made something good in response to the greatest challenge a mortal faces. That may not be good enough for you: it may not soften even a bit the fear we face. But it is the only kind of immortality we can imagine; at least the only kind we have any business wanting. That is a religious conviction if anything is. It is available to you whichever of the two camps of religion, godly or godless, you choose to join.

NOTES

1. Religious Atheism?

1. Albert Einstein, in *Living Philosophies: The Reflections of Some Eminent Men and Women of Our Time,* ed. Clifton Fadiman (New York: Doubleday, 1990), p. 6.

2. "Hymn to Intellectual Beauty" (1816).

3. William James, *The Will to Believe and Other Essays in Popular Philosophy* (New York: Longmans, Green, and Co., 1896), p. 25.

4. *United States v. Seeger,* 380 U.S. 163 (1965).

5. *Torcaso v. Watkins,* 367 U.S. 488 (1961), fn. 11: "Among religions in this country which do not teach what would generally be considered a belief in the existence of God are Buddhism, Taoism, Ethical Culture, Secular Humanism and others. See *Washington Ethical*

Society v. *District of Columbia*, 101 U.S. App. D.C. 371, 249 F. 2d 127; *Fellowship of Humanity* v. *County of Alameda*, 153 Cal. App. 2d 673, 315 P. 2d 394; II Encyclopaedia of the Social Sciences 293; 4 Encyclopaedia Britannica (1957 ed.) 325-327; 21 id., at 797; Archer, Faiths Men Live By (2d ed. revised by Purinton), 120-138, 254-313; 1961 World Almanac 695, 712; Year Book of American Churches for 1961, at 29, 47."

6. Richard Dawkins, *The God Delusion* (Boston: Houghton Mifflin, 2006), p. 8.

7. See Ronald Dworkin, *Justice for Hedgehogs* (Cambridge, MA: Belknap Press of Harvard University Press, 2011), chap. 8, "Conceptual Interpretation."

8. William James, *The Varieties of Religious Experience* (New York: Modern Library, 1902), p. 47.

9. Those who want to explore this objection and my response more deeply should look at Dworkin, *Justice for Hedgehogs,* chap. 2, "Truth in Morals."

10. Richard Dawkins, *Unweaving the Rainbow: Science, Delusion and the Appetite for*

Wonder (Boston: Houghton Mifflin, 1998), p. xi.

11. Rudolf Otto, *The Idea of the Holy* (1917), trans. John W. Harvey (Oxford: Oxford University Press, 1958), p. 7.

12. David Hume, *A Treatise of Human Nature* (1739–1740), bk. 3, pt. 1, sec. 1.

13. Paul Tillich, "Science and Theology: A Discussion with Einstein," in Tillich, *Theology of Culture,* ed. Robert C. Kimball (New York: Oxford University Press, 1959), pp. 130–131.

14. Ibid., p. 130. For discussion of the disagreement between Einstein and Tillich, see Max Jammer, *Einstein and Religion: Physics and Theology* (Princeton, NJ: Princeton University Press, 1999), pp. 107–114.

15. See Benedict de Spinoza, *Ethics* (1677), pt. 1, "Of God."

16. Steven Nadler, " 'Whatever Is, Is in God': Substance and Things in Spinoza's Metaphysics," in *Interpreting Spinoza: Critical Essays,* ed. Charlie Huenemann (Cambridge: Cambridge University Press, 2008), p. 69.

17. Stuart Hampshire, *Spinoza and Spinozism* (New York: Oxford University Press, 2005), p. 19.

18. Nancy K. Frankenberry, ed. *The Faith of Scientists: In Their Own Words* (Princeton, NJ: Princeton University Press, 2008), p. 222.

2. The Universe

1. In *Living Philosophies: The Reflections of Some Eminent Men and Women of Our Time,* ed. Clifton Fadiman (New York: Doubleday, 1990), p. 6.

2. Brian Greene, *The Elegant Universe: Superstrings, Hidden Dimensions, and the Quest for the Ultimate Theory* (New York: W. W. Norton, 2003); Anthony Zee, *Fearful Symmetry: The Search for Beauty in Modern Physics* (Princeton, NJ: Princeton University Press, 2007); Bruce A. Schumm, *Deep Down Things: The Breathtaking Beauty of Particle Physics* (Baltimore: Johns Hopkins University Press, 2004).

3. Greene, *The Elegant Universe*, p. xi.

4. Steven Weinberg, *Dreams of a Final Theory* (New York: Pantheon Books, 1992), p. 90.

5. John Keats, "Ode on a Grecian Urn" (1820).

6. Compare Hilary Putnam, *Ethics without Ontology* (Cambridge, MA: Harvard University Press, 2004), p. 67, where he discusses "value judgments that are internal to scientific

inquiry itself: judgments of *coherence, simplicity, plausibility,* and the like."

7. Stephen Hawking and Leonard Mlodinow, *The Grand Design* (New York: Random House, 2010), p. 7.

8. Marcelo Gleiser, *A Tear at the Edge of Creation: A Radical New Vision for Life in an Imperfect Universe* (New York: Free Press, 2010).

9. David J. Gross, "Symmetry in Physics: Wigner's Legacy," *Physics Today,* December 1995, p. 46.

10. Brian Greene, *The Fabric of the Cosmos: Space, Time, and the Texture of Reality* (New York: Vintage, 2005), p. 225.

11. Bertrand Russell and F. C. Copleston, "A Debate on the Existence of God," in *The Existence of God,* ed. John Hick (New York: Macmillan, 1964), p. 175.

12. Richard P. Feynman, *QED: The Strange Theory of Light and Matter* (Princeton, NJ: Princeton University Press, 1985), p. 10.

13. George Musser, *The Complete Idiot's Guide to String Theory* (New York: Alpha Books, 2008), p. 188.

14. Weinberg, *Dreams of a Final Theory,* p. 135.

15. This view is defended at length in my book *Justice for Hedgehogs* (Cambridge, MA: Belknap Press of Harvard University Press, 2011). I include these remarks only to show how the argument of this chapter melds with the arguments of that book.

16. Weinberg, *Dreams of a Final Theory,* p. 135.

17. Henry James, *The Ambassadors,* preface to the New York edition (1909), in James, *Literary Criticism,* vol. 2 (New York: Library of America, 1984), p. 1308.

3. Religious Freedom

1. UN General Assembly, Resolution 217A (III), "Universal Declaration of Human Rights," December 10, 1948.

2. Council of Europe, "Convention for the Protection of Human Rights and Fundamental Freedoms," November 4, 1950, Article 9(2).

3. John Locke, *A Letter Concerning Toleration* (1685).

4. Universal Military Training and Service Act of 1948, 50 U.S.C. Appx. § 456(j) (1948).

5. *United States v. Seeger,* 380 U.S. 163 (1965).

6. See Ronald Dworkin, *Freedom's Law: The Moral Reading of the American Constitution*

(Cambridge, MA: Harvard University Press, 1996), p. 101.

7. "Draft Declaration on the Church's Relations with Non-Christians," in *Council Daybook* (Vatican II, 3rd Sess., 1965), p. 282, quoted and cited in *Seeger*, 380 U.S. at 181–182 and n4.

8. Dworkin, *Freedom's Law*, p. 108.

9. *Planned Parenthood of Southeastern Pennsylvania v. Casey*, 505 U.S. 833 (1992). The three justices (O'Connor, Kennedy, and Souter) said that a woman's views about the permissibility of an early abortion fall into that category of conviction. They did not say that freedom of choice about abortion is protected by the First Amendment's free exercise clause—that would not have been possible, given precedents circumscribing that clause—but their opinion suggests the possibility that but for those precedents religious freedom could be understood as protecting the kind of convictions they described.

10. For a discussion of the opinions of the European Court of Human Rights, see George Letsas, "Is There a Right Not to Be Offended in One's Religious Beliefs?," in *Law, State and*

Religion in the New Europe: Debates and Dilemmas,
ed. Lorenzo Zucca and Camil Ungureanu
(Cambridge: Cambridge University Press, 2012),
pp. 239–260.

11. *Torcaso v. Watkins,* 367 U.S. 488 (1961).

12. The Supreme Court held that the First
Amendment does not require an exemption
from the ban on hallucinogenic drugs.
*Employment Division, Department of Human
Resources of Oregon v. Smith,* 494 U.S. 872 (1990).

13. See Laurie Goodstein, "Bishops Say Rules on
Gay Parents Limit Freedom of Religion," *New
York Times,* December 28, 2011.

14. Thomas Nagel, "Public Education and
Intelligent Design," *Philosophy & Public Affairs*
36, no. 2 (2008): 187–205.

15. See Ronald Dworkin, *Justice for Hedgehogs*
(Cambridge, MA: Belknap Press of Harvard
University Press, 2011), chap. 17, "Liberty."

16. On this test, however, Britain's "establishment" of the Church of England as official
religion does not offend ethical independence
if it is only a historical relic with no bite.
Consider the ease with which the ancient rule
establishing primogeniture in the

constitutional law of succession is being abandoned. There is no discriminatory life left in the old rule.

17. Religious Freedom Restoration Act of 1993, 107 Stat. 1488 (1993).

18. The *Smith* decision outraged the public. Many groups came together. Liberal groups (like the American Civil Liberties Union), conservative groups (like the Traditional Values Coalition), and other groups, such as the Christian Legal Society, the American Jewish Congress, and the National Association of Evangelicals, joined forces to support the Religious Freedom Restoration Act, which would reinstate the *Sherbert* test that overturned laws that burden a religion. The act, which was Congress's reaction to the *Smith* case, passed the House unanimously and the Senate 97 to 3 and was signed into law by President Bill Clinton. It was later held unconstitutional as applied to states. See *City of Boerne v. Flores,* 521 U.S. 507 (1997).

19. See Ronald Dworkin, *Life's Dominion: An Argument about Abortion, Euthanasia, and Individual Freedom* (New York: Alfred A. Knopf,

1993), and Ronald Dworkin, *Is Democracy Possible Here?* (Princeton, NJ: Princeton University Press, 2006). The abortion issue is more complex than I suggest in the text, because my opinion rests on the judgment, which I defend in those books, that a fetus does not enjoy rights of its own before an advanced stage of neural development.

4. Death and Immortality

1. I am quoting myself, from *Justice for Hedgehogs* (Cambridge, MA: Belknap Press of Harvard University Press, 2011), pp. 198–199.

INDEX